HELEN M. STEVENS'
EMBROIDERER'S YEAR

David & Charles

*For Steve, and all my friends, who
can make a year seem like a day.*

And in memory of Tess (Plate 42, page 65).

A DAVID & CHARLES BOOK

David & Charles is a subsidiary of F&W (UK) Ltd.,
an F&W Publications Inc. company

First published in the UK in 2004
Text and designs Copyright © Helen M. Stevens 2004
Photography and layout Copyright © David & Charles 2004

Distributed in North America
by F&W Publications, Inc.
4700 East Galbraith Road
Cincinnati, OH 45236
1-800-289-0963

A catalogue record for this book is available from the British Library.

ISBN 0 7153 1584 6

Executive commissioning editor Cheryl Brown
Desk editor Ame Verso
Copy-editor Lin Clements
Executive art editor Ali Myer
Book designer Sarah Underhill
Photographer Nigel Salmon

Printed in China by SNP Leefung
for David & Charles
Brunel House   Newton Abbot   Devon

Visit our website at www.davidandcharles.co.uk

David & Charles books are available from all good bookshops; alternatively you can contact our Orderline on (0)1626 334555 or write to us at FREEPOST EX2110, David & Charles Direct, Newton Abbot TQ12 4ZZ, UK (no stamp required UK mainland).

Plate 1 (previous page) Late autumn is the perfect time go looking for feathers. Shown from left to right: partridge, common jay, cock pheasant and mallard drake.
Shown larger than actual size
15.25 x 11cm (6 x 4½in)

Plate 2 (opposite) A mini sampler of techniques. Honeycomb stitch, split stitch and radial work describe the blue butterfly, its lower wings outlined by fine surface couching. The wings of the bumblebee and glow worm, in fine silk, metallic thread and blending filament, illustrate the variety of textures that can be achieved using a simple straight stitch.
7.5 x 7cm (3 x 2¾in)

CONTENTS

Plate 3 *(this page and cover illustration)*
Embroidery is the perfect medium to illustrate
the passing seasons of the natural year.
Beginning bottom left and clockwise:
spring – apple blossom and snowdrops;
summer – poppies, corn, dandelion and dog rose;
autumn – blackberries, traveller's joy and
hawthorn leaves;
winter – mistletoe, holly and ivy.
Embroidery shown life-size
26.5 x 20.25cm (10$\frac{1}{2}$ x 8in)

Plate 4 *(opposite) The Christmas robin in*
miniature forms an enchanting little subject
for an oval pendant.
5.5 x 4.25cm (2 x 1$\frac{3}{4}$in)

HELEN M.
STEVENS

INTRODUCTION

'Sunrise, sunset, sunrise, sunset:
Swiftly fly the years . . .
One season following another.'
('Fiddler on the Roof' Sheldon Harwick)

As each year turns we look forward to the ever-changing seasons – both in our own traditions and anniversaries and in nature. These can be as simple as a celebration of the harvest or as deeply meaningful as Easter and Christmas, as universal as the rites of spring or as special to one nation as Thanksgiving Day or Guy Fawkes' Night.

Embroidery, by its very nature, is a time-consuming art: any project demands that the embroiderer set aside time – that most precious of 21st-century commodities – time to plan, to design, to stitch. The very process of stitching can concentrate the mind on a happy subject, such as when working a wedding sampler or decorating a christening robe; or relieve grief and anxiety – the mourning pictures of the 19th century sustained many a grieving widow through the interminable and rigidly maintained months and years of black crêpe and lace.

Maybe it is this correlation between the embroidery itself and the time it takes to create it that has, through the centuries, led to the traditional use of embroidery to commemorate and celebrate all of life's most meaningful moments. Embroidery has always been used to enhance ritual and ceremony, from the pomp of a royal coronation to the intimacy of a baby's baptism. Rich robes and costly embroidered gowns are essential to every great event; simple folk embroidery and national costume are integral elements of country customs. Samplers chart the day-to-day home life of generations.

As our self-made anniversaries pass, so the natural life of the countryside rolls on with the passing of each season (see Plate 3). The icy gauze of winter melts into the velvet warmth of summer and inspires artist and embroiderer alike to capture each new phase before it passes on to the next. In this book I have explored each month in embroidery from the vantage point of traditional and more modern celebrations, as well as through the progress of the natural year. Whether you are seeking ideas for a special Christmas decoration or a summer birthday gift, I hope that there will be something here to inspire and excite you.

Welcome to my 'Embroiderer's Year'.

'the very process of stitching can concentrate the mind on a happy subject'

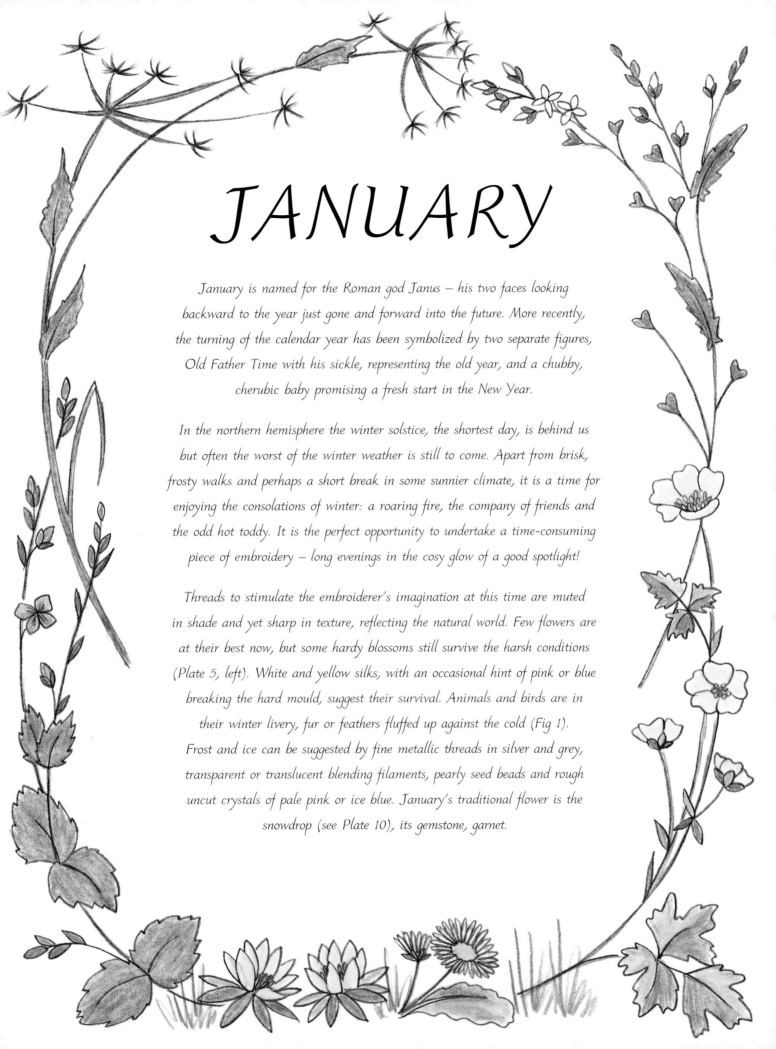

JANUARY

January is named for the Roman god Janus – his two faces looking backward to the year just gone and forward into the future. More recently, the turning of the calendar year has been symbolized by two separate figures, Old Father Time with his sickle, representing the old year, and a chubby, cherubic baby promising a fresh start in the New Year.

In the northern hemisphere the winter solstice, the shortest day, is behind us but often the worst of the winter weather is still to come. Apart from brisk, frosty walks and perhaps a short break in some sunnier climate, it is a time for enjoying the consolations of winter: a roaring fire, the company of friends and the odd hot toddy. It is the perfect opportunity to undertake a time-consuming piece of embroidery – long evenings in the cosy glow of a good spotlight!

Threads to stimulate the embroiderer's imagination at this time are muted in shade and yet sharp in texture, reflecting the natural world. Few flowers are at their best now, but some hardy blossoms still survive the harsh conditions (Plate 5, left). White and yellow silks, with an occasional hint of pink or blue breaking the hard mould, suggest their survival. Animals and birds are in their winter livery, fur or feathers fluffed up against the cold (Fig 1). Frost and ice can be suggested by fine metallic threads in silver and grey, transparent or translucent blending filaments, pearly seed beads and rough uncut crystals of pale pink or ice blue. January's traditional flower is the snowdrop (see Plate 10), its gemstone, garnet.

FROST AND FRESH BEGINNINGS

'Old Apple-tree, old Apple-tree,
We wassail thee and hope thou wilt bear . . .
Three bushel bag fulls
And a little heap under the stair!' (Traditional rhyme)

As midnight approached on Christmas Eve 1752, a great restless crowd gathered at the ancient site of the Abbey at Glastonbury in southern England to watch the 'sacred thorn'. This small, shrubby tree was reputedly a descendant of the thorn that sprang into life from the staff of Joseph of Arimathea when he brought Christianity to the island within a few decades of the Crucifixion. Each Christmas, quite out of its natural season, it burst into flower. But this year nothing happened.

As many of the waiting crowd had feared, supernature was adhering to the 'old' calendar – the Julian calendar, which had been in use in most of Western Europe since the 6th century. The Gregorian calendar, which had been introduced by Pope Gregory XIII in 1582 (to rectify some awkward anomalies to do with leap years), had been accepted by Catholic Europe for almost two centuries, but Protestant England would have nothing to do with it, until by the middle of the 18th century, England was 11 days behind the rest of the 'civilized' world. A more confident Church and the State then decreed that these 11 days should be sliced from the calendar, bringing England in line with the rest of Europe.

'don't be afraid to experiment with textures'

Fig 1 Even in the depths of winter there are certain visitors one can always count on! Bags of seeds or nuts attract tits, in this case the blue tit, within range of a handy window. Make a quick sketch (triangles are the theme here, see also Plate 63, page 96 and Fig 47, page 99) and take the inspiration back to your drawing board. At embroidery stage don't be afraid to experiment with textures – the rough netting of the bag could be suggested with a red 'fragmented' cotton.

Plate 5 (page 6) A cold, frosty morning: the spiders' webs are still encased in their sparkling jackets of hoar-frost and a couple of yesterday's unwary gnats, caught dancing in the winter sunlight, are about to provide an unexpected snack for the coal tit (Parus ater). Shepherd's purse (Capsella bursa-pastoris), the creeping buttercup (Ranunculus repens) and germander speedwell (Veronica chamaedrys) are all flowers that produce an occasional, errant bloom even in the depths of winter. Embroidery shown life-size 23.5 x 15.25cm (9¼ x 6in)

Simple folk, however, rioted in the streets believing that they were robbed of 11 days of their lives, and the recognition of traditional dates that were bound to the natural year by the threads of folklore and ritual were thrown into confusion.

At Glastonbury, blossom appeared on the sacred thorn on 5 January 1753 – the first day of Christmas by the old calendar, now however, Twelfth Night. A wise man, therefore, would follow the example of the thorn: traditional rites and ceremonies would have to change their official date to keep in pace. Consequently, the proper date on which to 'wassail' the apple trees and seek the blessings of the spirits of tree and field would be henceforth 16 January – the eve of Twelfth Night, old style!

It would be wrong to suggest that such a bureaucratic decision would significantly influence the observance of folk ritual for long. Some dates might be altered to fit the new framework; some would slip imperceptibly back to their original days and others would progress seamlessly, ignoring the new fads for their own timeless ends. At wells and springs, ribbons and threads would still be hung at the turn of the year to flutter like prayer wheels from one celebration to the next. The winter flowering of the Glastonbury thorn is still an annual miracle and our 21st-century New Year revels still cling to their long-forgotten and much-altered roots of ritual song, dance and colour. In Plates 6 and 7 I have tried to capture the ancient and modern of such celebrations.

Against a plain black background the ethereal snow-white blossom of the Glastonbury thorn bursts into life. The hawthorn (*Crataegus monogyna*) has a number of subspecies: 'Biflora', Glastonbury's 'magic' variety, is still to be found growing wild elsewhere in Somerset,

Plate 6 The hawthorn has more mystic associations than almost any other shrub and spans both pagan and Christian ideology. It was an integral part of the ancient Rites of Summer – normally blossoming around May Day in the unreformed calendar. To the early Christian converts of Western Europe it suggested the 'Crown of Thorns', one of the instruments of Christ's Passion. Bringing May blossom into the home was to court ill luck and to destroy a hawthorn was believed to bring untold disaster on the miscreant. The winter moth is a scourge of apple orchards – wassailing the orchard was thought to keep natural as well as supernatural misfortune at bay. 19 x 8.25cm (7½ x 3¼in)

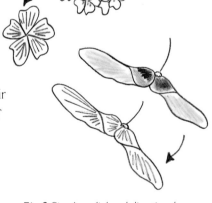

Fig 2 Simple radial and directional opus plumarium (see pages 132–3) describe the flowers and leaves of the hawthorn, working, respectively, towards a central or an elongated core. The two techniques are brought together in the winged seeds of the maple, the inner area (around the core of the seed itself) in radial work; the blade of the 'helicopter' wing in directional stitching toward the elongated core formed by the line of attachment to the seed.

Plate 7 Ancient northern European mythology held that the whole of creation was bound together by the threads of destiny and it has been suggested that modern celebratory traditions, from ticker-tape parades to the throwing of streamers, is a folk memory of this belief. Here, the natural and abstract have been brought together. A fine gold thread has been couched along the outer edge of the 'ribbon', omitted where the fabric reflexes against itself as it flutters to earth. Grasses interweave with both the ribbon and the natural elements of the design, pushing through the honeycomb of the dead leaf and engaging in a 'before/behind' interlace with plants and grasses.
11 x 11cm (4¼ x 4¼in)

its showy flower heads with their scarlet pollen masses giving way later to dark, wine-red fruits. Plate 6 is a simple study using elementary stitching techniques – as befits embroidery encapsulating the earliest design features of the year. Graduating stem stitch describes the stems and twigs, *opus plumarium*, both radial and directional (Fig 2), the flowers and leaves, and more open radial work captures the delicate sweep of the winter moths' wings. This pale golden-brown moth (*Operophtera brumata*) is on the wing from October to January and is often caught in car headlights – an apparently odd apparition as one edges gingerly between the snowy hedgerows of a winter's night, carefully negotiating the return from a New Year's Eve party.

'a brisk New Year's Day walk reveals the natural world's ephemera'

The following morning, however, all is bright and fresh and a brisk New Year's Day walk reveals the natural world's ephemera together with the cheerful detritus of the previous evening's celebrations (Plate 7). This study was suggested as I strolled past the garden of a 16th-century oak-timbered pub – paper hats and streamers lay scattered on the lawn, garlanding the daisies and filigree-veined oak leaves. This is a more complicated study of textures – simple radial and directional *opus plumarium* has been used for the natural features, together with honeycomb stitch (see page 25) for the striped leaf, whilst the coiling ribbon is worked in laddering (see page 51). This is a useful technique to create the impression of a woven effect (or on natural subjects a chequer-board pattern) and is worked by a form of needleweaving. The last element of this study is the winged seeds of the Norway maple (*Acer platanoides*).

The Norway maple has only been a resident species in Britain for the last 300 years. It was introduced into town parks and later landscaped gardens for its glorious autumnal colours which persist in its fallen leaves and seeds, if protected, into the depths of winter. The helicopter-bladed fruiting bodies fall spiralling to earth in September, but in a sheltered spot may lie virtually unchanged for months – they reminded me in this instance of a bright Christmas cracker trinket forgotten in the aftermath of a party. With the seeds as the 'core' of the feature, radial *opus plumarium* falls back towards them, shadow lines contouring between seed and wing (see Fig 2).

Plate 8 Phallic symbols of fertility were important in the dead days of winter and are evident here on both horse and carousing rider in a design taken from a Viking gravestone from Tjangride, Gottland. Plough Monday, the first after Twelfth Night, saw the intricately woven and often finely adorned symbolic (and feminine) 'corn dolly' laid in the newly ploughed field to be brought back to life by the (masculine) force of the earth. Texture and tactile elements are an important part of this 'New Year' study.
16 x 16cm (6¼ x 6¼in)

Fig 3 I have used the Anglo-Saxon Futhorc to create the runic inscription hidden in Plate 8. Here, the 29 symbols in red are each given their phonetic equivalent below. Our own language, of course, is different to that of the Anglo-Saxons but a little magical and artistic licence goes a long way (as Tolkein revealed with his own runic creation in The Lord of the Rings*) and these can provide an effective embroiderer's alphabet.*

The Norway maple is, as its name implies, a native of northern Europe and the harsh climactic conditions of mountains and fjords have made it very hardy and resistant to frost. Its wood is virtually indistinguishable from that of sycamore and can be used for a variety of purposes, from decorative to functional. The Vikings, whose exploration and exploitation of Europe during the latter half of the first millennium would have been familiar with its properties. Many a maple drinking vessel would have been raised to the turning of the seasons.

It is in the nature of one's own life to create personal and family traditions. My own love of embroidery means that whatever the season of the year and however hectic the celebrations, I must have some stitching 'on the go' – something that, if necessary, I can pick up and put down at a moment's notice, in between basting the turkey or uncorking the Champagne! Every Christmas and New Year I create a piece of work that takes on its own identity and evolves almost of its own will. Such a piece is Plate 8. Exploring textures such as those in Plate 7 made me think of trying to suggest different artistic media, from stonework to weaving, and a study of Viking art suggested this design. Textiles found in Viking ship burials and detailed stone carvings were its inspiration and hidden amongst the meandering, surface-couched black and gold plied thread of the background are runes in red silk: 'Odin and Sleipnir New Yearing'.

The outlines of the main features – the Norse god Odin on his eight-legged horse Sleipnir, and the surrounding border of tusked sea creatures – are worked in fine stem stitch: deep, mordant red, orange and green shades echoing the dyestuffs available in the 7th century. A series of surface techniques then add texture; very finely surface-couched silver thread within the central figures, more substantial couching within the main border and seed-stitched specking in gold thread to fill the border itself. The runes are simply worked in straight stitching. Runes evolved as a method of writing using only straight lines that could be

'my own embroidered "signature" has developed rune-like qualities over the years!'

Plate 9 *The fragile, friable stems of the previous year's cow parsley are a valuable design element at this time of the year (see also Plate 5). Whether encased in a sparkling wrap of frost or starkly etched on a plain background, the starburst patterns enhance almost any study. Worked in fine and graduating stem stitch tipped by straight stitching, it is a simple device to master (see Fig 5), but remember to superimpose foreground features to break up long, otherwise uninterrupted stalks as these can look dull and artificial. Here, the fluffy outer fringes of the squirrel's tail lightly overlap the main stem before the dense element of the tail obliterates it completely.*
15.5 x 13cm (6 x 5in)

Fig 4 A few quick squiggles create a squirrel! Always carry a few crayons and a small note pad with you and don't be concerned with details at this stage – they can be added later with reference to a good textbook – just get the feeling of the subject. Smooth, rounded contours are the theme here. When the design was adapted into its final form (Plate 9) I changed the directional sweep of the cow parsley to create a better framework for the main element.

easily carved into wood or chiselled on to stone. They make an ideal phonetic embroiderer's alphabet (see Fig 3). My own embroidered 'signature' has, I realize, developed rune-like qualities over the years!

Nature herself lies mostly dormant through January in the northern hemisphere. Hibernating animals are still deeply asleep and whilst a few hardy plants still produce the odd out-of-season flower, it is a mainly a time to conserve energy and await the coming of longer days and warmer nights. Animals that stored food during the previous autumn now seek out their hoards – for fresh food is in short supply. One such forward thinker is the red squirrel (*Sciurus vulgaris*). Unable to go without food for more than a few days, squirrels are often seen in midwinter, oblivious to an audience, excavating their hidden treasures – nuts, beechmast and acorns. Favourite hiding places are used again and again: young saplings representing previous years' unclaimed riches give a clue to current hiding places. Wait quietly by such a young tree and you may be rewarded, as I was,

by the sight of a squirrel foraging for breakfast (Plate 9). This deserved a quick sketch (Fig 4). Many venerable oaks began life in this way: strange to think that the timbers of the old pub I passed may well have been the result of some forgetful squirrel's hoarding some 700 or more years ago.

Succeeding strata of radial *opus plumarium* converging on the nose serve to build up the body of the animal. His tail, however, requires more elaboration. The skeleton beneath is quite a slim, whippy affair, but his glorious plume is made up of fine fur, thicker toward its core, more ethereal at the extremities.

Work inner, base strata first and then feed outer strata into this key area.

If possible, use a thicker gauge of thread toward the core and finer strands at the extremities (see Fig 5 and Plate 69, page 106).

Grasses, though having few fresh shoots at this time, are still useful to soften a design. Dull greens, old golds, beige and mossy shades of olive and aubergine suggest the half-life of these perennial waysiders. In Plates 5, 7, 9 and 10 straight, slightly angled stitches converging toward their base, or the bases of attendant features, provide a framework for primary elements of a picture – in the case of Plate 10 leading the eye down to the clear and rose quartz crystals: icy fragments amongst the aconites (*Eranthis hyemalis*) and snowdrops (*Galanthus nivalis*). Snowdrops were once known as the 'fair maids of February', referring to the folk custom celebrated on 2 February by the maids of villages who wore them as a symbol of purity for the Feast of the Purification of the Virgin. Reckoned by the earlier calendar, this would have been a January festival, perhaps derived from a pagan source. By either time-scale it was a step forward into the last month of winter . . .

Fig 5 Before beginning to stitch, analyse the various elements of your design (top) and if it helps, sketch out the stitch format in exaggerated format (bottom). You can refer to this later when the embroidery is underway. In filling techniques, always work the central areas first, working from the tip down in linear stitching. If you have a variety of gauges of thread remember to use finer strands to describe the more ethereal details.

Plate 10 This simple study captures the essence of midwinter and yet looks forward to the coming spring. A minimum of stitching has been used to suggest the ground – a few straight horizontal stitches in white stranded cotton and an equally sparse upright element of grasses. Rough quartz crystals nestle in the greenery of the aconites' foliage, the blue-green leaves of the snowdrops thrusting upwards, sinuous snake-stitched fields of contrasting colour.
10.25 x 7.75cm (4 x 3in)

Plate 11 A birthday, of course, can come at any time of year. To celebrate this winter birthday, brightly coloured maple leaf buds support a web in which the frosty initials 'CAL' have been picked out in blending filament and tiny ice-coloured seed beads.
16.5 x 12cm (6½ x 4¾in)

FEBRUARY

February has been called the restless month. Named for the Roman festival of purification, 'Februa', in the 5th century BC, it was the last month of the year. Calendar changes then placed it after January and it acquired the dubious honour of a varying duration – the odd six hours of each year added together are tacked on to February every fourth, or leap, year. Christian traditions followed the Romans in designating 2 February as Candlemas Day and it was dedicated to the Purification of the Virgin, with the pagan festivals of 'Lupercalia' and the Celtic 'Imbolc' (now metamorphosed into Valentine's Day) celebrating mating and fertility. The latter was a lambing festival and many farmers still arrange that lambing begins at this traditional time.

With the true warmth of spring still weeks away, the sight of early lambs nevertheless has the effect of lightening the end of winter, just as the lengthening days seem a promise of the season to come. Bulbs begin to shoot and some flowers, usually small and low growing, brighten the hard ground. The hellebore (Plate 12, left) is one of the few large-flowering plants to be at its best at this time, its pungent scent attracting and reviving the earliest bumblebees of the year.

In this strange transitional month we are drawn to a pale, luminous palette, echoed by an occasional deep shade within the same family of colours: violets (February's traditional flower) vary from icy-white through amethyst (February's gemstone) and delicate mauve to purple, while greens can suggest silver or dark jade.

STRANGERS, LOVERS AND FRIENDS

'I am raggedy,
You are fine,
But please still be my Valentine.'
(Traditional rhyme)

Fig 6 The cheerful, cheeky little chipmunk is a familiar sight in American parks and gardens – and much beloved of Walt Disney, of course. A quick sketch such as this could easily be adapted into an embroidery design: give yourself plenty of detail on face, paws and so on but play down the tail at drawing board stage – by adding a final fine embroidered strata in a single strand of silk this becomes the larger, fluffier appendage we expect.

It has occasionally been argued that the best thing that can be said for February is that it is the shortest month of the year! Certainly, in the northern hemisphere, it can seem interminable as the last of winter drags past and farmers know that as the days lengthen, much of winter's coldest weather may still be to come. 'In the barn on Candlemas Day should be half your straw and half your hay' advised rural folk in Europe, and the tradition of citing 2 February as an auger of weather to come was taken by the early settlers to North America.

Groundhog Day (now immortalized in film) is actually a far more ancient tradition than many people realize, dating back to the Romans. As the Legions marched into northern Europe, they took their belief that if the sun shone during the festival of *Februa* six more weeks of winter would follow. The Teutonic tribes took this prediction to heart and concluded that if a shadow was cast on 2 February spring would still be a long way off. A wise animal such as the hedgehog, would therefore, on seeing his own shadow, promptly return to hibernation. Pennsylvania's earliest settlers were German and finding

'Groundhog Day is an ancient tradition dating back to the Romans'

Plate 12 (page 16) The woodland floor in late winter is a surprisingly busy place. The wood mouse (Apodemus sylvaticus) does not hibernate (although its metabolism slows down to survive food shortages) and by February it is already looking for a mate. The sweet violet (Viola odorata) is the only violet to have scented flowers, and in less sanitary days was the first flower of the year to be available to sweeten linens that had become musty over the long damp months of winter.
Embroidery shown life-size 25 x 19cm (9³/₄ x 7¹/₂in)

Plate 13 'How much wood would a
woodchuck chuck, if a woodchuck could
chuck wood?' As a child in the United States,
my favourite tongue-twister celebrated the
exploits of Punxsutawney Phil – though
unlike beavers, the groundhog does not build
lodges or dams but blocks its burrow through
the roughest weather with thick grasses and
wood chips. In common with most small
animals, the core of the subject is the nose,
towards which all the stitches should fall (see
also Fig 28, page 61). The sweep of the
trillium frond, which softens and frames
this study, creates the impression of a much
closer foreground by voiding between the
lower leaves and the background features.
Voiding can be a useful tool on a pale fabric
as well as on a black one.
21.5 x 13.25cm (8^1/$_2$ x 5^1/$_4$in)

Plate 14 *Known to generations as the emblem of a brand of boot polish, the kiwi is a delightful little bird, rarely glimpsed in the wild. Its closest relative appears to be the long extinct moa, also of New Zealand, but strong national pride in this fellow assures its continued survival. As a nocturnal subject it is best portrayed on a black background, though its rather dull colouring means that the picture needs to be 'lifted' by the introduction of bright greenery and lively textures.*
8.25 x 10cm (3¹/₄ x 4in)

no hedgehogs in their adopted country, transferred the honour of this arbitration to the groundhog, otherwise known as the woodchuck. The town of Punxsutawney is now established as the home of Phil, the famous groundhog who is consulted each 2 February: if, on emerging from his burrow he sees his own shadow and returns to his sanctuary, the worst of winter is still to come; if not, spring has arrived!

The groundhog (*Marmota monax*) (Plate 13) may well deserve its reputation for wisdom as it can live for over 15 years. A relative of chipmunks (Fig 6) and squirrels (see January Plate 9, page 13), it is among the largest of the marmot family, at up to 80cm (31in) long, surviving the winter on a hoard of seeds, nuts, dried berries and other plant food painstakingly gathered in the autumn and stored underground. Stocky and four-square, its ramrod-straight back and stubby nose make an interesting exercise in *opus plumarium* as strata of stitches swing abruptly from an east-west to north-south alignment. Compared with the gentle sweep of stitches on the woodmouse (Plate 12) this angular arrangement needs to be softened by subduing the voiding between each break of plane. The dense, thick fur is closely worked, only the whiskers breaking the outer contour of his coat.

'no bird has become more symbolic of its nation than the kiwi'

By the time the painted trillium (*Trillium undulatum*) (Plate 13) comes into bloom all threat of snow is passed, though the pinkish-purple sepals of the flowers have elements in common with the European hellebore (*Helleborus foetidus*) (Plate 12) which flourishes during the last throes of winter. Both are woodland plants, the latter protected to a certain extent from the worst of the weather by its secluded habitat. Working the petals' purple arcs in Dalmatian dog technique and flooding the strange green shade around these markings creates the luminous effect of these bell-shaped blooms.

'a few goldstone pebbles add a final three-dimensional touch'

Deep in woodland on the other side of the world, the kiwi (*Apteryx australis*) (Plate 14) is enjoying summer during February, just as its human compatriots are celebrating their national holiday. Waitangi Day, 6 February, commemorates the signing of the Waitingi Treaty when the European settlers became fully established in their new homeland. No bird on Earth has become more symbolic of its nation than the kiwi. New Zealanders proudly refer to themselves as 'kiwis', and it appears on coins, stamps and a myriad of products both for export and internal consumption.

Kiwis are strangely unbird-like, roly-poly, flightless creatures about the size of a large chicken. The female normally produces an enormous single egg, often weighing up to a quarter of her body weight, which is then passed over to the male who single-handedly undertakes the long incubation period of up to 80 days. A disproportionately long bill is equipped with nostrils at its very tip allowing the bird to find its prey, mostly grubs and worms, amid the deep ground litter of the forest floor. Being nocturnal, the kiwi's sight is poor, but this is compensated for by long, tactile bristles at the base of the bill. Plate 14 is a study in texture, from these strange 'whiskers' and hair-like feathers to the soft ferns, mosses and grasses of the 'proper bush', as New Zealand's primeval forest is called (what is left of it).

Converging to an elongated point, the first stratum of stitching in fine floss silk is sharply angled to create the bill, subsequent strata becoming increasingly radial as

Fig 7 Work each frond of the ferns (top) in a line of stem stitching, always following the flow of the curve (middle). Remember the rule: needle in on the inside of the curve and out on the outside of the curve. The final sketch shows this rule extrapolated and much exaggerated to emphasize the direction of the stitches.

Plate 15 'This is the day the birds choose their mate, and I choose you, if I'm not too late.' In Devon, England, this little rhyming couplet was a traditional ditty for Valentine's Day and a perfect message to include in a card with this design. If an embroidery is to be mounted in a card, use a slightly lighter backing board than for framing (see Basic techniques, page 129) but still lace firmly to avoid puckering.
10.25 x 10.25cm (4 x 4in) including embroidered border

head gives way to body, each stratum subdued (as on the groundhog in Plate 13). The chalky-white egg is worked in straight stitching in twisted silk outlined in metallic silver thread, while grasses are in stranded cotton worked over and in front of stem-stitched ferns (Fig 7). Mosses to either side frame the picture, worked in meandering surface couching in bouclé silk and fine wool. A few goldstone pebbles add a final three-dimensional touch.

The middle of February brings Valentine's Day, a tradition now celebrated throughout the Western world. There are actually several saints sharing the name Valentine, two of whom also share 14 February as their saint's day. The commemoration of a pagan priest of the Roman gods, who succoured persecuted Christians, subsequently converted and was clubbed to death in AD270, together with his namesake the Bishop of Terni, who was martyred a few years later, happens to coincide with the eve of the Roman feast of *Lupercalia*. A feature of this celebration was the choosing of partners for the coming year by the drawing of lots – a concept that scandalized the Christian church, which tried, but failed, to suppress it. Tradition, however, insisted that mid February was the time when birds chose their mates and the custom of sending romantic (or lascivious!) anonymous gifts and messages died hard in rural communities. By the mid-Victorian era the practice had become a pretty charade between sweethearts and it remains popular today.

Plate 15 is an attractive design (interpreted again in Fig 8) which could make a delightful valentine for a loved one. The little bird could be replaced with another motif (Fig 8 offers alternative suggestions) and the surrounding heart worked in techniques of individual choice. Here, straight stitching, seed beads and surface-couched gold cord and metallic threads form a chunky border. A window mount has also been stitched in fine silk and gold threads ready for framing but the central design could simply be slipped into a blank or decorated window card to create a charming keepsake.

Fig 8 Little Tyrolean motifs make charming subjects for a valentine study. You can, of course, choose any colourway that appeals and by working successive bands around the outside of the heart, the design can be enlarged as far as you wish.

Plate 16 *Although both specific designs and colours are symbolic in Chinese iconography, they are often interchangeable. The 'pink bat of happiness' does not always appear to be pink. Imperial robes in yellow could be embroidered with blue 'pink bats' to give a more aesthetically pleasing effect. Could this be the origin of the nonsense expression 'sky blue pink'? At a time of the year when a little humour is needed to brighten the days, visual puns were also a favourite of the Anglo-Saxons (see December, Fig 58, page 123).*
17 x 12.5cm (6³/₄ x 5in)

'Chinese art seems to embody an ability to conjure up evocative designs for any season'

The Chinese New Year is celebrated in January or February by the Western calendar, during the coldest months of our winter. Chinese art seems to embody an ability to conjure up evocative designs for any season, and winter is no exception. The 'three friends of winter' (Plate 16) is the Chinese name for a trio of subjects that flourish in nature as well as in art at this difficult time of the year – the pine, bamboo and plum blossom. The twisted, gnarled effect of the pine bark (almost like a bonsai) is created by working directional *opus plumarium* – always flowing with the curve of the motif – in several strata of silver silk, lighter above and darker below, the meandering pattern of the stitches catching the light and emphasizing the differing shades. Sunbursts of straight stitches in fine metallic gold are centred

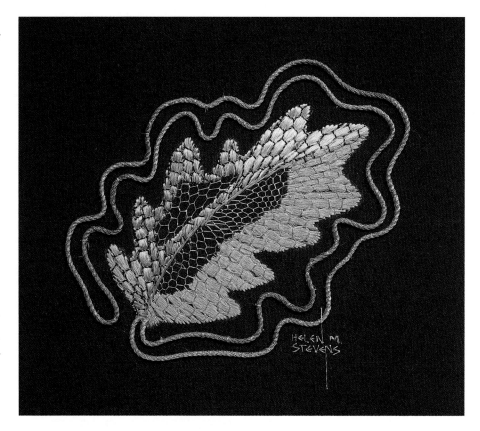

by mauve seed beads to suggest stylized cones, whilst beneath, in the shelter of the larger tree, the angular bamboo presents a contrast to the soft pink plum blossom, both worked in floss silk. The blossom, its colours and texture, are echoed by the strange little creature that flies over the scene: this is the pink bat of happiness, an enchanting, be-whiskered little fellow who traditionally it is hoped will accompany the coming of the New Year (Fig 9).

On the last day of February every four years, Leap Year's Day offers the opportunity for girls to take the initiative in matters of the heart. Once called 'The Ladies' Privilege', 29 February could be a very expensive day for an unfortunate male, for it was held to be impossible for him to refuse a proposal of marriage except upon substantial payment – a silk embroidered gown or a hundred guineas. Consequently, if a girl 'set her cap' for an unwilling boy he would do well to remain hidden throughout the day until sunset brought an end to his peril. The origin of these customs is still unknown, though certainly there is some

Fig 9 The Chinese pink bat of happiness is a popular motif in embroidery and other fine arts. The long curlicues issuing from its mouth can suggest either whiskers, or, more traditionally, the breath of well-being that the little fellow bestows upon his patrons.

connection with feminine superiority. One story is set in Ireland: St Bridget met St Patrick and complained that it was unfair for women not to have the right to propose marriage. St Patrick replied that this was the natural course of things but was harangued by St Bridget for so long that he conceded the right once every seven years. St Bridget was still not satisfied and bargained him down to one in four.

'a fallen oak leaf is worked partly in honeycomb stitch to suggest the intricate striped veining'

The ancient Greek Pythian games were also held every four years at Dephi, when the victors were awarded crowns of oak leaves. In Greco-Roman myth, the oak was sacred to Zeus/Jupiter and during the ceremony of marriage between Jupiter and Juno, devotees likewise wore oak crowns. When Mark Anthony thrice offered Julius Caesar the crown of Rome, Caesar refused saying, 'Jupiter alone is the King of Rome'. This event occurred during the ceremony of *Lupercalia*, which brings us neatly back to February. Plate 17 celebrates these ancient traditions.

In Plate 7 (January, page 10) a fallen oak leaf is worked partly in honeycomb stitch to suggest the intricate striped veining. This technique has been explored and exploited in Plate 17 to create a variety of textures in gold. The outline of the leaf (including the 'holes' at the centre and to one side) is transferred on to the fabric, the central vein worked in silk stem stitch. Directional *opus plumarium* then describes the two sides and widely spaced directional stitches are extended from the *opus plumarium* to the vein. Honeycomb stitch is then worked to fill the voids (Fig 10). Subsequently, the same technique is worked over the top of the *opus plumarium* to create a quilted effect suggestive of the dry, friable texture of the dead leaf. A thick gold cord is couched around the whole motif to suggest a necklet rather than a crown of oak for the man in your life. What more special way to celebrate this strange, transitional month?

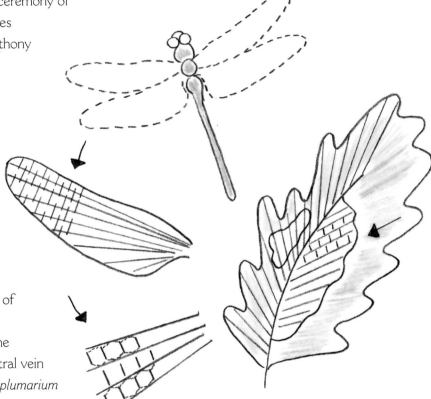

Fig 10 Honeycomb stitch is more obviously used on the wings of insects such as the dragonfly (left, top to bottom, and see also The Myth and Magic of Embroidery, *D&C, 1999) but it is also useful for dead, striped leaves (right). Work radial stitches towards the core of the subject (on a leaf this is elongated) and then lay a short stitch over two radial stitches at right angles and repeat, brickwork fashion. As the stitches are tightened the radial stitches will gradually be pulled in opposite directions to form the honeycomb pattern.*

MARCH

March often comes 'in like a lion', and its name commemorates its stormy associations. The Roman god of war, Mars, spoke through thunder and lightning whilst the Anglo-Saxon name for March was 'Hlyd Monath', the 'loud, stormy month'. Both St David's Day (1 March) and St Patrick's Day (17 March) fall within this month, although it is the patron saint of Wales rather than Ireland whose traditional flower is more symbolic of the season, for the daffodil encapsulates the spirit of spring.

Together with the primrose (Plate 18, left, March's associated flower, sometimes shared with February), the narcissus, in its many forms, is the true harbinger of warm weather. From the simple wild daffodil to the hybridized specialist flowers of many a country show, its trumpet-shaped blooms herald the spring equinox with a fanfare of colour and scent. Pollen is in the air, too, from many trees, especially willows, whose catkins and lamb's tails scatter the unwary with a yellow, powdery dust. The first butterflies are to be seen — unexpected scraps of bright gauze fluttering in the still dusky hedgerow, where the dogged, year-round flowers of the red deadnettle are suddenly eclipsed by the vibrancy of young growth.

The colours of spring are light and airy; textures are soft and delicate. Now is the time to add to your collection of fine threads. Single strands of silk worked into tiny seed stitches create the diaphanous effect of pollen-tipped filaments, while soft grey threads suggest the cat-like, silky fur of the pussy willow. A sheen of pastel green is evocative of the immature leaves of many plants, whilst aquamarine (March's gemstone) suggests light spring rain.

DAFFODOWNDILLY

'So many mists in March,
So many frosts in May.' (Traditional country saying)

Fig 11 Imagine a flower pulled apart into its separate sections, then work each petal or part thereof in radial opus plumarium *falling back towards the core – which is the point at which all the sections converge.*

Although March winds and April showers are still ahead of us before we are advised to 'cast our clout (cloak)' at the end of May, the arrival of the first month of spring is a welcome milestone on the way to warmer weather ahead. As early buds begin to swell, nature's larder becomes less bare and her colours become those of the dairy – all yellow and white, clotted cream and buttermilk, with textures increasingly warm and frothy.

One of the first butterflies on the wing is the brimstone (*Gonepteryx rhamni*) (Plate 18), whose butter-coloured wings are thought to have given the whole genus its common name. This species, which can be on the wing for as much as ten months out of the twelve, are soon followed by other 'whites' (Plate 19), the green-veined white (*Artogeia napi*) (top) and the small white (*Artogeia rapae*) (below), much maligned by kitchen gardeners but still pretty additions to the immature hedgerow.

Both Plates 18 and 19 capture the feel of early spring. Light and airy, almost sparse in design, they suggest that there is much more to come later in the year, but are full of the promise of the new season. The goat willow (*Salix caprea*) is better known as the pussy willow, its soft grey catkins sleek as the fur of any oriental feline and later, yellow, pollen-bearing male flowers as fluffy and

'as with all floral embroidery, finding the "core" or "growing point" of the bloom is all important in creating a successful interpretation'

***Plate 18** (page 26) It is unusual to picture a butterfly in flight from below – the underwing is generally less attractive than the upper surface – but the delicate brimstone is as pretty from this aspect as any other. The brick-red spots are rudimentary false eyes to scare off predators, a necessary defence when there are so few other insects on the wing to draw their attention. Apart from the few low grasses, this study is worked entirely in floss silk: textures are varied by the different application of the stitches.*
Embroidery shown life-size 24 x 17cm (9½ x 6¾in)

Plate 19 *As flower arrangers know, daffodils are stiff, unforgiving subjects in the flesh, and in embroidery, too, they need careful handling. Both standard petals and trumpet are inflexible, but the depth of the troughs at the centre of the flower and the curving, elegant extremities need to be given a feel of waxy strength rather than a wooden quality. Use a dark, deep grey to suggest the dense shadows, switching abruptly to the yellow of the flesh. Allow the directional sweep of the stitches to give a feeling of movement; only change to a lighter shade of silk for the reflex of the petals.*
16.5 x 9.5cm (6¹/₂ x 3³/₄in)

Daffodowndilly - March 29

bouffant as the most pampered Persian. Both of these effects are achieved with fine silk thread, the former worked in shades of silver, graduating from pale above to darker beneath in slightly elongated seed stitches, the latter with tiny speckling stitches superimposed in yellow gold to effect an aura of minute dots. By contrast, both the hybridized Poet's Narcissus (*Narcissus poeticus*) and the wild daffodil (*Narcissis pseudonarcissus*) are worked in bold long stitching.

'the colours of spring are light and airy; textures are soft and delicate'

As with all floral embroidery, finding the 'core' or 'growing point' of the bloom is all important in creating a successful interpretation (see Fig 11). Once the core is established and the radial *opus plumarium* has a 'home' to approach, the stitching converges smoothly, stitches slipping beneath their neighbours to avoid overpacking at the centre (see page 131). Plate 20 brings this bold stitching together in a simple, colourful design, concentrating on radial and directional *opus plumarium*. Always work inner strata first, on the pansy and butterfly. On the former, the outer strata can then be worked around the inner, shooting stitches superimposed later to give the 'bee-line' tracery. On the brimstone, remember to work the Dalmatian dog spots before flooding in the rest of the wing. Simple, centrally veined leaves are worked in directional *opus plumarium*. For a more detailed exploration of this type of work, see *Helen M. Stevens' Embroidered Flowers* and *Embroidered Butterflies*, D&C, 2000 and 2001.

St David's Day (1 March) is all to do with youth and new beginnings. Seemingly born to the holy life, he effected his first miracle whilst still an infant: as his mother, St Non, held him to be baptized by a blind bishop, the baby splashed holy water into the bishop's eyes, thus restoring his sight. Generosity seems to have been his watchword and his saint's day conferred the same blessing. If a farmer had not managed to plough his fields by 1 March, his neighbours would rally round to help: coming with ploughs and oxen, they would complete the work, accompanied by their wives who would cook for the entire company. Apparently leeks were an integral ingredient of the pot – it is not recorded whether daffodils played any part!

The name daffodil is very old. According to Greek legend, it derives from the name of a plant that flowered in the Underworld, and its springing to life from the barren ground so early in the year echoes part of many pagan life-death-rebirth beliefs. Confusingly, one of its country names is the 'primrose peerless', although there is no family connection with primulas. The *primula* (Fig 12), meaning 'first rose', naturally acquired its name also from its habit of early flowering and is the subject of a number of country customs.

Coming into bloom at the same time of year as the hatching of poultry, and both primroses and chicks being bright yellow, it was believed there was a link between the two. Children were warned never to bring less than 13 primroses into the house, as this was the optimum size of a clutch of eggs – fewer flowers meant less chicks would hatch. Recipes survive from the 1400s for 'prymerose potage', a rich, celebratory pudding of almonds, honey, saffron and ginger, and heady primrose wine made in the early spring was drunk in the autumn to perpetuate the onward roll of the seasons.

Like the daffodil, the primrose can be worked simply in radial *opus plumarium* for the flowers and directional *opus plumarium* for the delicate, wavy-edged leaves. Countless hybrids are grown in the world's gardens, including the specialist auriculas. These have become something of a

'St David's Day is all to do with youth and new beginnings'

Fig 12 The primrose (Primula vulgaris) *(centre),* cowslip (Primula veris) *(right) and false oxlip* (Primula veris x vulgaris) *(left) are all closely related members of the primula family – their leaves almost identical. The latter is, in fact, a hybrid of the first two, primrose-like flowers apparently emerging from cowslip sepals. In these days of less wide-spread wildflowers such a cross is rare but charming and can be found most often where the two parent flowers grow in close proximity.*

Plate 21 Like tulips (see Fig 17, page 40), auriculas have been the subject of colour plates and prints for centuries. Their almost military qualities of perfection and precision give them an unreal dimension – only the bumbling flight of the white-tailed bumblebee (Bombus lucorum) brings a touch of reality to this study.
9.5 x 8.25cm (3³/₄ x 3¹/₂in)

cult flower with innumerable variations of petal pattern and colour, the more rigidly defined the better (Plate 21). Nurtured and cross pollinated by enthusiasts, all these variants derive from a single species found in the European Alps in the 16th century, and being alpine plants require clear, cool growing conditions; many keen gardeners overwinter them in frames.

In common with all simple, radially worked flowers, begin stitching with the innermost strata, progressing steadily outward, always taking your stitches towards the growing point (Fig 13). A measure of the perceived perfection of the real flower is the abruptness of change between one colour and the next. This can be very successfully imitated in embroidery by creating a distinct 'cut' between different coloured strata, as on the yellow and purple flowers. The harlequin pattern of the outer strata on the lower flowers can be worked by using two needles at the same time. Thread both, with appropriate shades, and using them alternately work your way around the motif. 'Park' whichever needle and thread is not in use away from the stitching, to the top left of your work if you are right-handed (conversely top right if you are left-handed), keeping them away from the tools in use to avoid tangles.

St Patrick's Day is 17 March (shared with St Joseph of Arimathea), a date much celebrated both in Ireland and the United States, where, thanks to wholesale immigration from Ireland after the terrible famines of the 19th century, Patrick is almost as popular as he is in the Emerald Isle. The

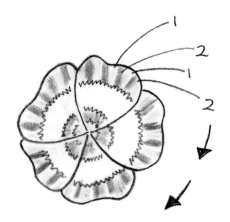

Fig 13 Having worked the inner three strata of the auricula in yellow, orange and white, a final harlequin strata can be worked with two needles. Work each stripe in succession (red, yellow, red, yellow: 1, 2, 1, 2,) keeping to the usual rule of stitching from the outside inwards. Any appropriate colourway may be chosen.

traditional St Patrick's Day parade in New York is a riot of green. Green, of course, is the second colour of spring, for as the yellows begin to pale, a thousand shades of green take over as new leaves and grasses of every variety suffuse the countryside. Plate 22 is a landscape dedicated to the emerging foliage of the season. Tiny pinpricks of green gather along branch and twig in the hedgerow, and trees create a tracery of gold-green against the sky. None is more beautiful and elegant than the silver birch (*Betula pendula*).

'tiny pinpricks of green gather along branch and twig in the hedgerow, and trees create a tracery of gold-green against the sky'

The silver birch was sacred to the Celtic and Germanic tribes of Europe; in Britain the Druids believed that it possessed powers of purification and renewal, both important elements of the spring festivals. This belief persisted into the era of well-recorded history, when 'birching' was the favourite means of punishment for delinquents: the choice of birch switches arose directly from the belief that beating with birch could drive out evil spirits.

Plate 22 *A pastel green circular window mount would display this study to best effect, drawing the eye deep into the countryside to a point along the projected route of the running hare. The ploughed field breaks the flow of green upon green, and a suggestion of sky adds a further dimension. The bulk of the landscape is worked in horizontal straight stitching, broken only where the fields 'disappear' behind a fore- or middle-ground feature.*
10cm (4in) diameter approximately

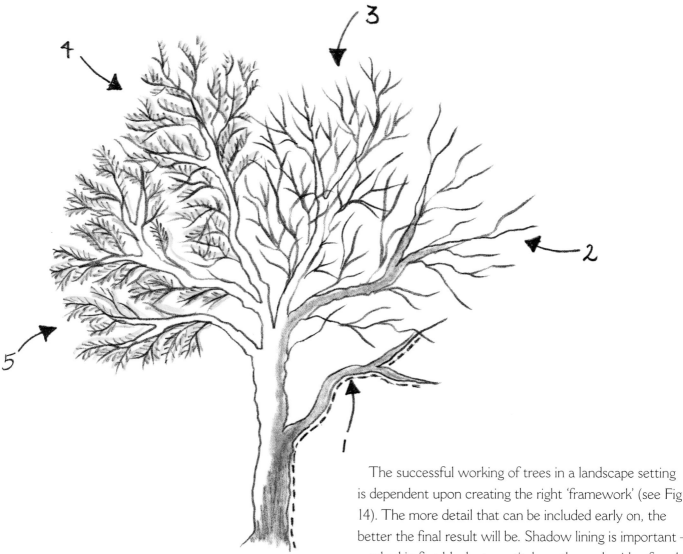

Fig 14 The more effort you put into the working of a tree, the better will be the result: time consuming, but true. From the right: (1) shadow line only under 'two-sided elements' such as the trunk and major boughs, (2) stem stitch the branches emerging from the larger boughs, (3) add twigs in straight stitch to the branches, (4) 'clothe' the twigs with leaves, lighter above and (5) darker below.

The successful working of trees in a landscape setting is dependent upon creating the right 'framework' (see Fig 14). The more detail that can be included early on, the better the final result will be. Shadow lining is important – worked in fine black stem stitch on the underside of each 'two-sided' element, i.e., trunk and large boughs, while smaller branches and twigs need only suggest the play of light and shade through choice of colour. Early spring trees are not clothed with leaves as densely as those later in the year (see Plate 36, pages 54/55), and small leaves often bunch together. This can be suggested by working seed stitches 'across' the flow of the twigs, as though individual features had all merged into one delicate, trembling mass.

'there is no more enchanting a sight than hares scampering helter-skelter across an open field'

One of the clichés of spring is the Mad March Hare. It is not known why brown hares (*Lepus capensis*) become particularly boisterous in March and April (hormones are not a factor as they breed all year round), but perhaps it is simply the *joie de vivre* of the season. There is certainly no more enchanting a sight than one or more

hares scampering helter-skelter across an open field. Suggesting such a scene in miniature is a challenge. As in full-sized animal portraiture, the sweep of radial stitches must fall towards the head of the subject but, clearly, working on such a small scale limits the number of stitches to be used. Work in as fine a thread as possible, remember to shadow line and don't be afraid to overemphasize slightly the important features – almost as though creating a slight caricature. Certainly at the distance from which we are viewing the hare in Plate 22 we would not really be able to see his whiskers, but to suggest them with a few fine stitches draws us into an intimacy with the subject. Experiment with a few rough sketches first (Fig 15).

Fig 15 Even in a very loosely sketched form the differences between rabbits (above) and hares (below) can be noted. A very quick sketch 'in the field' is enough to give you inspiration when you get back to the drawing board but even then you need not include too much detail. The 'caricature' style of a small, descriptive piece allows for impressionism in your stitching, as in your sketching.

The last week of March takes us beyond the vernal equinox (in the northern hemisphere) and into the period when daylight outlasts night. Together with the summer and winter solstices, the spring and autumn equinoxes were important turning points in the pagan year.

In the style of 8th-century Anglo-Saxon gold and silk work I have created a series of embroidered plaques to commemorate each (Plate 23, see also Plate 41 page 65, Plate 68 page 105 and Plate 80 page 123). Here, the sun and the moon appear together, a domestic fowl and trefoil foliage (like the shamrock of St Patrick, a symbol of both pagan and Christian unity) beneath the configuration. Outlined first in red stem stitch, the design is then infilled with a jigsaw of colours in split stitch. Finally, the gold and silver metallic thread is surface couched, coiling from the outside of each motif inward, like springs ready to burst.

Heralded by a lion, March's traditional final fanfare is that accorded to a lamb. But a few quiet days are all that the countryside can allow, for with the approach of April, all nature begins to gather its resources for the frenetic activity to come.

Plate 23 Although apparently random, the jigsaw effect of split-stitched colours is intended to convey a stylized landscape. The lower half of the design concentrates on darker, deeper shades, including green, whilst the upper includes pale blue and gold; a daylight sky to the sun side of the sun/moon motif, and dark blue and buff, the night sky of the moon side. This is a modern evolution of a Saxon design concept.
6.25 x 5cm (2¹/₂ x 2in)

APRIL

'Omnia aperit' cried the Romans as April, the fourth month, 'opened all things'. Spring truly comes to fruition during this month as new life, rebirth and the endless cycle of the seasons are resurrected. Easter most often falls within April, Christian tradition again following pagan ceremony as the various gods of mirth and youth rejoiced with the welcome arrival of warmth and well-being. The Celtic god of humour, Lud, Roman Saturnalia and the medieval Feast of Fools all conspire to be recalled in the more modern tradition of April Fools' Day.

All is frenetic activity within the natural world. With the coming of lighter mornings, the dawn chorus becomes a cacophony of blended bird calls as early nestlings pipe their endless demands for food. Deep in burrows and sets, mammals more peacefully suckle their young, whilst in wood and hedgerow buds burst, leaves unfurl and caterpillars munch their way through the myriad of the season's delicacies.

Now is the time to add colour to your palette of threads. Those bright lime greens, pulsating pinks and enigmatic shades of mauve and purple suddenly seem less foreign and more attuned to the vibrancy of youth. Surprisingly, there are even seeds to be found in spring – the goldfinch relies on dandelions and other perpetually fruiting flowers to provide extra nutrition (Plate 24, left) – so even bright and old golds have their place. April's gemstone is the diamond, a prism through which every colour and angle is emphasized; its flower is the daisy, its year-long blooming cycle just a part of high-spring's ongoing celebrations.

JESTERS AND HEROES

'Midday, midday, long gone past
And you're the biggest fool at last.' (Traditional rhyme)

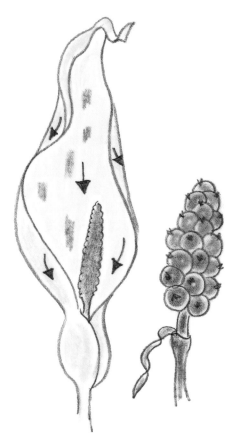

Fig 16 As with most plants the core of the flower and its surrounding elements is where the 'business' is going on – where the reproductive organs of the plant are to be found. In the case of Lords and Ladies this is at the base of the spadix. Work all the elements of the hood, both in straightforward radial opus plumarium *and in opposite angle stitching, as though they are falling back towards this growing point (left). The colourful berries (right) succeed the spadix later in the year.*

With the coming of April, the innocence of early spring begins to give way to boisterous buffoonery. The true origins of April Fools' Day, the first of the month, are lost, but certainly were well known in the 1600s when it was celebrated as 'fooles' holy day', a day when the simple and mischievous were given full rein. Like the Lord of Misrule at Christmas, the King of the Fools could do no wrong, but only until midday when his authority was lost – hence no April fool pranks are valid after noon.

The cuckoo comes in April, another harbinger of foolishness as it lays its eggs in other birds' nests, making 'cuckolds' of its hosts. At the same time, the cuckoo pintle or cuckoo pint (*Arum maculatum*), with all the sexual innuendo attendant upon its suggestive anatomy, blooms. So, too, flowers the early purple orchid (*Orchis mascula*), from which a potent love potion was brewed as late as the last century in both Ireland and the Shetland Islands. Taken to North America in the 17th century, this 'amorous cup' was said to have 'wrought the desired effect' just as successfully in the New World.

The woodland floor in April (Plate 24) is a place where one could well believe that such mayhem and magic is commonplace: strange shapes and colours riot and the

'with the coming of lighter mornings, the dawn chorus becomes a cacophony of blended bird calls'

Plate 24 (page 36) A group of goldfinches (Carduelis carduelis) is called a 'charm' and what, indeed, could be more charming? Four to six eggs are laid in April or May and chicks are hatched around two weeks later. After another two weeks they leave the nest but are still dependent upon their parents for another week while they learn the tricks of the trade. Catching thistledown or dandelion seeds in flight must be quite a challenge to a fledgling. Working black against black can be made easier by always using a good light, allow voiding to outline individual feathers and, if necessary, add a few very fine white highlights – such as here on the head. Embroidery shown life-size 26.5 x 19.25cm (10½ x 7½in)

trees are alive with birdsong. Against a black background the luminous qualities of the subject are seen to their best advantage. Both the early purple orchid and the arum lily (cuckoo pint) have vibrant green foliage spotted with mauve blotches, lightly speckled on the former, broader and deeper hued on the latter. In embroidery these may be described in separate ways: the delicate marking on the long, sword-like leaf of the orchid may be superimposed on the underlying directional *opus plumarium* in small groups of ticking stitches; the larger spots of the lily leaf are worked in Dalmatian dog spots, the deep purple shades worked first, the green then flooded in around them.

The flowers of both plants are extraordinary. 'Lords and Ladies' (yet another name for the cuckoo pint) have a strange purple spadix above a cluster of male and then female flowers (all on the same plant, see Fig 16). It is the female flowers that when fertilized develop into the familiar red berries seen later in the year. The early purple orchid has an even more remarkable anatomy: each flower has three inner and three outer petals, the upper five combining together to form a hood which invites pollinating insects to enter; the lower petal forms a landing pad which bounces visitors against the pollen-bearing stamens, so pollinating the flower. All of these complex fascinating features can be effectively worked by determining the 'growing point' of the subject and, with simple and opposite angle stitching, using radial *opus plumarium* to describe the various curves and reflexes.

The garden as well as the countryside really begins to come to life in April. The Pasque flower (*Pulsatilla vulgaris*) (Plate 25) is more often seen now in gardens than in the wild, though originally it was most often discovered growing around Roman ruins, prompting the theory that the Romans introduced it to the British Isles. Flowering around Easter time gave it its common name (not to be confused with the passion flower), though it is likely to have had some significance to the Romans in their Saturnalia (spring) festivals, a tradition which, like many others, may have slipped into the Christian era. At Easter, Pasque flowers were boiled in

Plate 25 *The pretty Pasque flower is one of my garden favourites. As soon as the fine green leaves emerge, I know spring is really here, then the fat purple buds open and the flowers form a tossing mass of colour in the wind. When the flowers die back, silky seed heads appear, staying on the plant for several weeks; rather like traveller's joy, these seed heads could be worked in floating embroidery (see Fig 45, page 94).*
9.5 x 5.75cm (3³/₄ x 2¹/₄in)

'the garden as well as the countryside really begins to come to life in April'

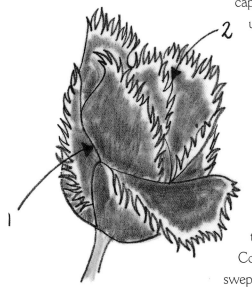

Fig 17 As a rule of thumb, the width of your void depends on the gauge of your thread. The thread should just be able to nestle in the little valley created by your voiding. Hence, working in a fairly bold gauge for the main body of the petal, the void would be quite wide (1), whilst where the feathery effect is created by the use of a much finer thread, the void will be proportionately narrower (2).

water with eggs to turn the eggs green. This simple study captures the silky feel of the flower: thick sleave silk is used to recreate the density of the petals and converging stem stitches to describe the deeply serrated quality of the leaves. Offset by the single reflexing blade of an emerging tulip leaf, this would make a delightful design for an Easter card.

Taking over from the daffodils, which are the staple church decoration for an early Easter, tulips are their showy successors. Tulips have been prized garden flowers for centuries. They were first brought to Britain in 1554 and at around the same time they arrived in Europe from Constantinople (now Istanbul). Suddenly 'Tulipomania' swept the aristocracy, with fortunes made and lost on the promise of a single bulb – one *Semper Augustus* bulb changed hands for 13,000 guilders, a king's ransom in today's money. From these early specimens all the current hybrids arose: single, double, cottage (with long, pointed petals), parrot (curled petals splashed with green or other colours) and, more recently, fringed (Plate 26). I could not resist the challenge of these extraordinary blooms.

'Fleshy' is the best way to describe the texture of the tulip – both flower and leaf. Here, the inner surfaces of the leaves have been worked in a plied silk, which has been untwisted and then put back together loosely to achieve an almost padded effect within the *opus plumarium*. Smooth floss silk is worked for the stems and outer surfaces of the leaves. Thick floss silk (the whole unsplit gauge of a Japanese skein would be ideal) describes the main body of the petals; inner strata worked first as appropriate, leaving a broad 'river void' between each petal (see Fig 17). In a much finer floss silk (approximately one third of the original width), short arcs of stem stitch are worked to create each strand of the fringe. Allow these to converge or diverge as necessary to create the random, frilly effect, but carefully feed the base of each line into the radial work of the main petal to achieve a smooth transition from one texture to the next.

Most garden species of tulip bloom somewhat later than their wild relatives, and this is also true of the many

'tulips have been prized garden flowers for centuries'

Plate 26 *Most flower arrangers know the tip of making a hole through the stem of a tulip, about 2.5cm (1in) below the flower head, to stop the bloom drooping. I have a better one: with your needle take a thread right through the stem and loop several flowers together. Nestling amid foliage, you cannot see the thread but the flowers cluster together much more easily than as individuals – embroidery and flower arranging combined!*
19 x 9cm (7¹/₂ x 3¹/₂in)

Fig 18 *Meandering surface couching can be as random as you choose but remember that as you change direction, there must always be a couching stitch at the angle of the turn (top) to hold the main thread in place securely. The rule still applies where a fluffy thread is used (below). Don't be afraid to displace the fragmentary fibres as this will add to the naturalistic effect of the piece. Emphasize this fluffing up by lightly teasing the finished piece with a baby's toothbrush.*

Plate 27 *Cherry plums still grow along the banks of the River Blackwater in Essex, England and on Northey Island in the estuary. In autumn their fruit flashes blood-red in the sunshine, and it was here that Brithnoth, Ealdorman of Essex was killed by the Danes in AD991 at the Battle of Maldon. His wife, Aelfthryth, was a noted embroideress and might well have recognized these motifs – for their story see* The Myth and Magic of Embroidery, D&C, 1999. *14.5 x 9cm (5³/₄ x 3¹/₂in)*

flowering cherries. Whilst the wild cherry plum (*Prunus cerasefira*) is in full flower almost before winter is over, the purple-leaved cultivar 'Pissardii' blossoms when its leaves are at their prettiest slighter later in the year, their frothy pale pink flowers and glossy red foliage a welcome contrast to the waxy, contrived perfection of the tulips. Compare Plate 26 and Plate 27 to see what a diverse range of effects can be created by working basic techniques in a variety of gauges and applications. There are times, however, when we must rely on a completely different approach, alternative materials and a juxtaposition of these and traditional techniques to create an altogether original study (Plate 28).

'That's the wise thrush; he sings each song over, lest you should think he never could recapture the first fine careless rapture', wrote Robert Browning in his poem 'Home Thoughts from Abroad'. 'Oh, to be in England, now that April's there . . .' There is, indeed, a very special magic in the finding of an

Plate 28 *Spring's dawn chorus is really the song thrush's finest hour. With a huge repertoire of calls and trills, a single song can last up to five minutes, detailed phrases repeated at intervals as if truly 'composed'. The thrush* (Turdus philomelos) *enjoys human company and is often seen in parks and gardens, providing a good opportunity to study its speckled markings at close quarters. Dalmatian dog technique is the key to their successful working – each spot merging smoothly into its surrounding creamy ground.*
16 x 12.75cm (6¹/₄ x 5in)

occupied bird's nest. The golden rule, of course, is never to disturb the occupants, but once spotted, and watched quietly from a respectful distance, there is no more thrilling an experience than to witness the growth and fledging of the family. An empty bird's nest at the end of the season is well worth studying to gain an insight into the method of its construction.

'the portrait of a large, handsome bird does not need additional gimmicks'

All species have their own tricks and techniques, from the apparently haphazard construction of a pigeon's nest – a few sticks jammed into a fork or platform in a shrub – to the intricately packed, mossy mass of the robin's nest. I had both in my garden as this book was written.

Now is the time when those oddly textured threads that you could not resist ('they'll come in handy one day . . .') really come into their own. I have used a variegated, slightly bouclé mohair yarn to create the thrush's nest in Plate 28. This has been surface couched (see Fig 18) in a meandering

Plate 29 *Here is Australia's famous laughing kookaburra. The plumage of this delightful, plump bird is softened on the head, back and breast by working a final fine strata of silk, just overlapping the outline at exactly the same angle as the preceding strata. This gives an appropriate level of contrast to the completely smooth contour of the wing and tail feathers.*
15.25 x 10.75cm (6 x 4¼in)

continuous thread to form the cup, with a little dark shading towards the base and at the lip to give a three-dimensional effect. In Plate 28, mother and chicks appear to snuggle down into the nest's rough concavity. With a light brush – a baby's toothbrush is perfect – tease the surface of the wool in places to vary the texture further. The resulting nest is a very convincing suggestion of moss, dead grass, horsehair and other treasures.

The browns, buffs and creams of the song thrush provide her with a perfect camouflage, and although the same cannot be said for many members of the kingfisher family, the Australian kookaburra, the largest of the relatives, is one of the least gaudy (Plate 29).

ANZAC (Australian and New Zealand Army Corps) Day, 25 April, is the day when Australia and New Zealand remember the part their forces played in recent conflicts. If the kiwi is symbolic of New Zealand, the kookaburra (*Dacelo gigas*) (from the Aboriginal, pronounced cook'aburra) captures the very spirit of his home nation: from the jaunty set of his cap to his infectious laugh, he *is* Australia. For a kingfisher, his colours are somewhat subdued, but his habitat is harsh and he needs an element of surprise to catch his favourite prey of snakes and lizards. Snakes are approached from the rear, seized behind the head and carried off, either to a perch to be battered senseless by his huge bill, or to be dropped to their death from a great height. Either way his meal is assured.

The portrait of a large, handsome bird does not need additional gimmicks. There is enough interest in Plate 29 to hold the attention – both of stitcher and subsequent viewer (see Fig 19). Work radial *opus plumarium* converging upon the tip of the bill, strata merging, voided or softened as appropriate. The large blue feathers on the flank are worked first, voided slightly to their tip, with Dalmatian dog technique merging their bases to the fuller flow of the plumage. The large markings on the back are also Dalmatian dog – more diffuse markings added in clumps of ticking stitches. Shadow line and highlight carefully between the main feathers of the wings, and terminate strata abruptly to give the strong stripes of the tail.

April is autumn in Australia and animals and birds alike are beginning to prepare for the winter ahead. In the northern hemisphere the opposite is underway. St George's Day (23 April) past, it was traditionally said that the worst of April's showers were also behind. In Norfolk, England, Snap the Dragon (Fig 20) – apparently more important than the saint who slew him – snaps at the heels of summer, and in Wiltshire the 'Cuckoo King' was elected. The revels of May Day fast approach.

Fig 19 The Australian galah is a natural comedian. This delightful pink parakeet indicates its frame of mind by the use of its crest; lying flat suggests the bird is at its ease, while the further it is raised the more agitated the bird. The kookaburra (Plate 29) uses its crest similarly though much less obviously. Treat large feathers individually (see also Plate 1).

Fig 20 'Snap' the Norwich dragon is as old as the English tradition of St George. Much rebuilt and elaborated over the centuries, his 'skirt' hides the mummer beneath who, from within, operates the snapping mouth and flapping wings. Just a few days before the revelries of May Day, the lusty spring festivals have already begun!

MAY

May Day, despite the disapproval of both Church and State in
many countries of Europe, has stubbornly refused to be undermined.
May is named for the goddess Maia; her father, Atlas, bore the Earth
upon his shoulders, and the astronomical configuration of the Pleiades
represents Maia and her six sisters. The first of May (though temporarily
usurped by the Communists) is really a celebration of the feminine:
the May Queen or May Lady is the essence of fecundity – the 'green
gown of May' was a metaphor for what girls might receive
by lying on the grass with their lovers!

Everything about May seems to be an overt reference to love. The Maypole
(phallically symbolic), May Dew, said to make a girl irresistible, and the
May Baby (presumably the outcome of the two), were all part of the lusty
fun. In nature, too, the fruits of early spring matings are coming to light.
Birds' first broods are fledging, young animals are making their initial,
tentative forays into the wider world, and in the countryside and garden
alike more elaborate floral displays are on the way. With frosts hopefully
a thing of the past, the delicate water violet (Plate 31)
and magnolia (Plate 34) are a joy.

An ephemeral, transient month, May is the time to create delicate,
imaginative designs. Now comes the natural flowering of the may
(or hawthorn, May's associated flower, see also January Plate 6, page 9),
whilst its gemstone, emerald, reflects the many greens of late spring.

RIBBONS, BUTTONS AND BOWS

'May Day's breaking, all the world's awaking . . .
Sleeping in the daytime wastes the happy May-time.'
(Traditional rhyme)

Early Christian missionaries to pagan Britain, aware of the futility of trying to make their converts abandon their former customs and beliefs, successfully incorporated Christmas, Easter and All Saints' Day into the old gods' pastoral calendar – but they could never manage to subdue the riotous, lusty festival of May Day, the Celtic Beltane. In the 17th century, the Puritans intoned drearily against the licence of May Day, and it wasn't until the 20th century that controversies over certain lewd May-eve practices were finally resolved.

Certainly the coming of May heralds a certain frisson in the natural world. Activity moves up a gear; late-pairing animals and birds have finally made their choice of partners, and those creatures that produce several broods a year are by now on their second and becoming seasoned parents. Insects and plants reach maturity and make way for new generations. Along the river bank life is all aflutter.

The water vole (Plate 30) is 'Ratty' in Kenneth Graham's delightful and timeless book, *The Wind in the Willows*. Water voles mate for life and, like Ratty, seem to find 'nothing – absolutely nothing – half so much worth doing as simply messing about . . .'. Evidence of this is what they leave behind – a mass of half-eaten, toyed-with vegetation and frivolously extensive burrow systems with several entrances above and below the water line. Despite this

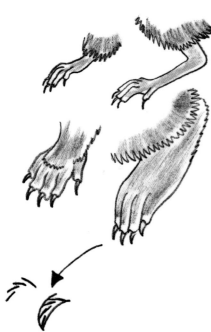

Fig 21 Large or small, most animals' feet have claws. These can be effected by working a few graduating stem stitches (see Stitch variations, page 132) in a short arc. These three or four stitches will meld together to create a convincing claw-like shape.

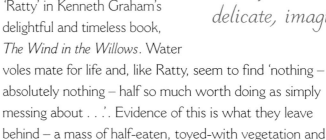

'May is the time to create delicate, imaginative designs'

Plate 30 (page 46) The water violet (Hottonia palustris) is the only member of the primrose family to be completely aquatic (and it isn't a violet at all). Above water it is entirely leafless, fine thread-like leaves growing beneath the surface. The plant's delicate tracery is an effective foil to the density of the study's main feature, the water vole (Arvicola terrestris). Compare this traditional method of treating the flowers with the more stylized effect of the ribbon embroidery in Plate 31. Embroidery shown life-size 25.5 x 20.25cm (10 x 8in)

Plate 31 This is a complete flight of fancy. At the centre of each loop-stitched ribbon flower is a creamy seed bead, superimposed over a couple of short straight stitches in yellow (refer to a good ribbon embroidery textbook). Gold thread highlights both leaves and mayflies and the billows of unspun silk are caught down with tiny green seed-beaded bugs. Cuckoo froth (or spit) is produced by the nymph of a minute green bug, the frog hopper, here somewhat glamorized by its beaded interpretation.
9 x 6.25cm (3¹/₂ x 2¹/₂in)

lifestyle, they can still manage to rear up to five litters a year. In days when fur was more sought after by the fashion-conscious the water vole was sometimes a victim of hunters, its dense, luxurious pelt rivalling mink in its softness – though with a head and body less than 20cm (8in) long, it is horrific to think how many skins would be needed to make a garment. This gorgeous fur does make a fine subject for radial *opus plumarium*.

The glossy, chestnut-chocolate coat is fairly uniform in colour and so careful shading is necessary, in addition to the sweeping, change-of-angle variations of the stitching, to create a realistic three-dimensional effect. Ratty is a tubby fellow and needs to appear rounded and stocky. With two shades of brown in a fine silk thread, it is possible to mix light and dark in the needle to give a subtle blending of paler and deeper colours. To vary the texture from fur to flesh on feet and tail, change to a single strand of stranded cotton. Add the final touches of claws in gunmetal grey silk – a few graduating stem stitches create a claw (see Fig 21) – and use fine black silk for straight-stitched whiskers.

Little black boot-button eyes are brought to life with a single white seed stitch. Always work the eyes before the surrounding facial fur as it is easier to work around a given feature than to leave a 'hole' to be filled with straight stitching later. Focus the eyes on a specific feature to give your picture a sense of reality and spontaneity (Fig 22). The object of this vole's attention is the sub-adult mayfly just emerged in front of him. Britain's largest mayfly (*Ephemera danica*) gives away the secrets of its lifestyle in its names. Appearing in May, this ephemeral beauty lives just one day in its adult form – though it has been two years beneath the water as a voracious nymph. The nymph climbs up a plant stem (bottom right Plate 30), sheds its skin once to become a dull sub-adult called a 'dun' (bottom centre), and then again to reach glittering maturity (above). I have worked it into a May Day fantasy in Plate 31.

Close to my cottage in Suffolk, England runs the River Lark, the meandering waterside path a favourite springtime walk. In May, the lady's smock (*Cardamine pratensis*) masses on its banks, gossamer threads of spiders' webs

Fig 22 Take a bead between two features of your subject's face: here, the eye and mouth are used as 'sights' for the converging lines. Place the object of your subject's attention at a point just beyond where these two lines converge – now you can be sure there's no mistaking his interest!

10.75 x 10cm (4¹/₄ x 4in)

Fig 23 The wings of the mayflies in Plates 30 and 31 are worked in straight, converging radial stitches in your finest available thread. Leave a little of the background fabric showing through the radial work, allowing the impression of movement, and work to just outside your transferred line. Long straight stitches also suggest the tail filaments and legs, with shorter stitches for antennae and so on.

stretching down to lower-growing herbs, and cuckoo froth festooning its stem. Dancing around the flowers, mayflies weave an intricate pattern, newly emerged insects testing their wings and males seeking females. This seemed to me the epitome of nature's maypole. Traditional village-green maypoles are topped with garlands and ribbons, so I thought an experiment with ribbon embroidery would be fun. Having transferred my design on to fabric in the usual way (see Basic techniques, page 128), the stems and leaves are worked in stem stitch and *opus plumarium*. Then narrow, pure silk variegated ribbon worked in two simple techniques creates the flowers and buds. From the flowers to the lower shoots, long straight stitches in cellophane thread suggest the cobweb tracery and raw, unspun silk arranged and lightly caught down, create the cuckoo froth.

It is not only in fresh water that the spirit of May shows itself in unlikely ways: on the coast the elegant avocet (*Recurvirostra avosetta*) (Plate 32) indulges in a strange ritual known as grouping or 'maypoling'. Pairs of birds (eggs are laid in April or May) group together in perfect circles to indulge in a ritual of confrontation. Mates press closely together, posturing and displaying in front of their equally exhibitionist neighbours. The behaviour appears to have no logical explanation. In the simple study in Plate 32, cellophane thread has been used again, this time to suggest the sun glinting on the water. Choose a blending filament (see Suppliers, page 136) with a transparent cellophane thread (this will be twisted with a more substantial, silk-based thread). Carefully separate out the former, discarding the base, and thread it into a fine embroidery needle. (It is essential that an embroidery or long-eyed needle is used, so the delicate cellophane thread, similar to a tiny flat ribbon, will pass through the fabric smoothly without snagging.) Work long straight stitches across the fabric, keeping them at an even tension with the background. Depending on your choice of a clear or coloured cellophane thread the result is either subtle or dramatic (see also Fig 23).

In the countryside of old, life and death were but two sides of the same intricate embroidery and even in lusty, life-giving May, mortality could not be completely forgotten. The fritillary or snake's-head lily (*Fritillaria meleagris*) (Plate 33) was also known as the lepers' lily because it bloomed when lepers (as the sufferers of Hansen's disease were called) were likely to be on a spring pilgrimage to find a miraculous cure. Its flower also looked like the bell rung by the unfortunate victim in order that the healthy might give him a wide berth. Once common in wet meadowland, it is now a rare sight in the wild, more often planted as a curiosity in gardens. The chequer-board pattern of the bell is worked in laddering (see also the coiling ribbon in January, Plate 7, page 10). To create the pale, upper surface of the petals, radial *opus plumarium* is worked, converging at the growing point where flower meets stem. A darker thread of the same gauge is then needlewoven through the stitching (but not

Fig 24 The process of laddering is quite straightforward. From the top, first work the petals in standard radial opus plumarium *from the outer edge towards the growing point. Then, with a darker shade, work a needlewoven thread through the surface of the stitching, at right angles to the underlying embroidery. Repeat this on each upper petal. For the lower petals, work the same sequence of stitching, with the darker thread used for the base embroidery and the lighter for the needleweaving.*

Plate 33 Snake stitch is an appropriate treatment for the long, sinuous leaves of the snake's-head fritillary. Working to the same principle as stem stitch, always bring your needle out on the outside of the curve to be described, and put it in on the inside. Where the field reflexes, begin at the centre, breaking the motif into two separate curves and work each separately (see Stitch variations, page 134).
9.5 x 9.5cm (3³/₄ x 3³/₄in)

the background fabric) at right angles to the original (see Fig 24). The colourway is reversed on the underside of the petals to give a negative effect.

The border of the May-flying Camberwell Beauty's wings (*Nymphalis antiopa*) (Plate 33) imitates another ribbon effect. The country names of this lovely butterfly, 'mourning cloak' and 'lace petticoat', refer to the outermost band of colour, but within, a blue and black pattern looks for all the world like a ribbon-embroidered, running-stitched hem. Here, however, the blue spots are worked in Dalmatian dog technique, black *opus plumarium* flooded around them, falling away to the mulberry-coloured inner strata.

In the Victorian language of flowers, the magnolia represented dignity, an apt choice, for botanists believe that magnolias are among the oldest plants in the world. Fossils over five million years old suggest that as the world's climate has changed, magnolias were once far more widespread than their current native range. Certainly they do not occur naturally now in Europe or Australasia (though are present in parts of eastern North America), but as imports they thrive under good conditions. In Britain their main enemy is the frost, so if blooms hold off until May they are usually safe. In my garden *Magnolia* x *soulangiana* (Plate 34) has a habit of flowering late and I feel that summer is fast approaching when its waxy-white petals stained with purple unfurl from their buds like satin bows unable any longer to contain a parcel bursting from within. The stamens and stigmas inside, often 'set' and strange banana-like fruits begin to grow, culminating in the autumn with the emergence of blood-red seeds. During the spring, however, these powder puffs of red and green gather dewdrops at their centre and a sparkling, creamy prism is created reflecting the petals.

In Plate 34 I have contrasted the long, bold stitching of the petals with tiny seed stitches at the core of the open flower and superimposed glassy seed beads to suggest water droplets. These have also been scattered at points on the buds and leaves. Like the tulips in Plate 26 (April, page 41) this is a bold, botanical study.

Plate 34 The dense petals of the magnolia must be worked in closely abutting stitches. Sweep the angle of the stitches gently (remember, the shorter the stitch that is slipped under its neighbour, the more abrupt the change of angle will appear) to ensure that there are not too many stitches vying for space at the centre of the flower. Recap your radial opus plumarium *technique in Stitch variations, page 133.*
17.75 x 13.25cm (7 x 5¼in)

Back in the wild, matters are progressing apace. Hedgehogs begin to breed in April, and at about four weeks old the young start to take solid food. Night-time excursions with their mother teach them what is and is not good to eat, with worms and caterpillars being favourite foods (Plate 35). Soon, the babies wander off alone to begin their rather solitary lifestyle. The young hedgehog's underfur is as soft as any animal's and when very small their spines (actually modified hairs) are useless. As they mature these become sharp, effective protection against predators. They are 'ticked' (their colour varies along the length of the spine) and this can be recreated in embroidery by working each prickle in three separate stages. Embroider the main features and fur of the hedgehog's pelage first, following the usual rules for the depiction of animals (see February Plate 13, page 19 and Fig 28, page 61). Now treat each spine individually: first work the upper edge of each in a pale grey, then create a chevron by working a lower straight stitch in dark grey angled to meet the first. Finally, in finer thread, work a single straight stitch in white through the chevron, extending beyond the tip. See Fig 25 for sequence. Massed together these elongated chevrons worked in three shades create the variegated effect of the ticked spines.

The hedgehog is Britain's only spiny mammal, and like the porcupine in America and echidna in Australia has much folklore associated with it. 'Off we go again, as the hedgehog said to the Devil!' was once a common country saying. The story goes that one May night a hedgehog made a bet with the Devil that he could outrun him racing up and down a ditch. The Devil took the wager and the hedgehog curled up into a ball at one end of the course and appeared to begin rolling along, while another hedgehog made a ball at the other end. The Devil dashed back and forth but whichever end he arrived at a hedgehog was waiting for him saying, 'Off we go again!'. The Devil became so tired that he slept through the whole of the year's sweetest month . . . June.

Fig 25 The prickles of the hedgehog are worked in three stages. (1) A long straight stitch is worked at the appropriate angle, establishing the flow of the prickles at drawing board and transfer stage. (2) Angle a second stitch in a darker shade to meet the first. (3) Work a finer white thread through the chevron created by the first two stitches, allowing it to extend beyond the existing tip.

JUNE

June is traditionally the month of midsummer revels, but it is also a busy month in the countryside, so celebrations were once confined to a short period around the summer solstice and Midsummer Day. The month is named for the Roman goddess Juno, wife of Jupiter. Her Greek equivalent was Hera, and the Norse incarnation, Freyja, 'The Lady'. All these personas were associated with fertility and growth – and in June the natural world's headlong rush into summer is indeed a time of breakneck activity.

For the embroiderer, June offers so much inspiration that it is difficult to decide upon individual themes. Colours are fresh yet vibrant, textures lively yet rich: the promise of ripeness is in the air but all is still young and immature. Now is the time to take a few crayons in primary shades out into the countryside and make bold, sweeping strokes of colour on rough paper (Fig 26). Capture just the essence of the day: hot, bright and active. Bring your sketch home and add the details in the cool of the long, light evening.

In the language of flowers both rose and honeysuckle (the traditional flowers of June, see Plate 37, left) represent love; the former in its purest form, the latter its unbreakable bonds, whilst the bitter-sweet nature of June is perfectly captured in its associated gemstones – moonstone and pearls. The ghostly, translucent qualities of both gems speak of the supernatural, of fairies and spells and short, bright, starlit nights. Suggest these qualities with fine, ethereal milky-white silks and rainbow-hued blending filaments; broaden your palette of greens and introduce delicate touches of metallic gold.

MIDSUMMER NIGHTS AND DOG-DAYS

'Barnaby bright, Barnaby bright:
The longest day and the shortest night.' (Traditional rhyme)

St Barnabas's Day, 11 June, traditionally marked the beginning of hay-making and we are still advised to 'make hay while the sun shines'. Before the alteration of the calendar in 1752, 11 June *was* the longest day and potentially the sunniest of the whole year. Midsummer Eve, now 23 June, along with similar celebrations in spring, autumn and winter, marked one of the pivotal points of the year, a few hours when the boundary between the natural and supernatural worlds was fragile and easily breached.

'now is the time to take a few crayons in primary shades out into the countryside'

Shakespeare understood this and his *A Midsummer Night's Dream* has mortals and fairies interacting to the amusement (albeit possibly nervous) of his sophisticated Tudor audience. On Midsummer Eve in London, Nottingham and other cities, a 'marching watch' was held when the townsfolk – usually sceptical of their country cousins' superstitions – patrolled the streets with portable braziers and protected themselves against the forces of the other world with ribbons and finely broidered jerkins.

Country folk, though cautious not to offend the 'little people', accepted them as part of the natural order and if on midsummer nights they could catch a glimpse of one it was considered a boon (Plate 38). Woodland was the

Fig 26 Although Midsummer Day officially falls within the month of June, it still feels very much like the beginning of summer and the riot of wayside colours can take us by surprise. Introduce yourself to the new season by taking a very few shades of vibrant pink and green on your inspirational forays. Concentrate on shape and form (as here) and add the subtleties of colour later.

Plate 37 (page 56) In late June the first of the new generation of peacock butterflies (Inachis io) appear – earlier in the season they may be rare, very late survivors of the previous year's hibernation. They patrol their woodland or hedgerow territories ferociously, making frequent aggressive sorties to investigate trespassing butterflies or other insects. The bright false eyes on the wings are intended to frighten predators, whilst a harsh rasping noise is produced by rubbing its wings together. Multiple Dalmatian dog is ideal to describe this complicated wing pattern – see also Helen M. Stevens' Embroidered Butterflies, D&C, 2001. Embroidery shown life-size 26 x 16.5cm (10¼ x 6½in)

Plate 38

'. . . a delicate cobweb canvas
That gleamed like a magic glass,
And bloomed like a banner of elf-land
Between two stalks of grass.'
('The Elfin Artist' Alfred Noyes)

Directional and radial opus plumarium, tiny seed stitches and
straight stitching are all that are needed to create this 'banner of
elf-land'. Oberon's mischief-making love potion, designed to make
Titania fall in love with whoever she first encountered, might well
have included periwinkle, for the herbalist Nicholas Culpeper
(1616–54) later stated, 'Venus owns this Herb, and saith that the
leaves eaten by Man and Wife together cause Love between them.'
21.5 x 16cm (8½ x 6¼in)

natural habitat of fairies and June, with the treetop canopy still letting sunlight and moonlight on to the woodland floor, was the time to look. Rapid plant growth at this time of year produces a tangled, interwoven mass of foliage and flowers (see also Plate 38) as honeysuckle, roses and periwinkle stud and star the wood with colour. Ferns, too, are growing rapidly; reproducing by scattering minute spores instead of seeds. These were believed to have supernatural powers for they were so small as to be virtually invisible and yet they obviously existed because they gave life to new ferns: gather them in the right manner at the right hour and you could acquire the cloak of invisibility.

Most European ferns produce deeply indented leaves which can be difficult shapes to render in embroidery. Like the dandelion leaf (Plate 39), the correct angle of directional *opus plumarium* that describes each side of the leaf is integral to successful working. Establish this angle by making a quick overlaid sketch on your original design (Fig 27). Imagine the leaf entire and establish the flow of stitches: include this directional flow within the outline of the fern (remember that whatever is included *inside* the parameters of the outline can be transferred on to your fabric as it will ultimately be covered by embroidery). Work each side of the leaf in turn, allowing the stitches to fall back to the elongated core of the central vein in the usual way. The common

Plate 39 *It is often said that 'the devil is in the detail'. Here, certainly, the impish quality of the stoat's mask is enhanced by the tiniest of additions: two white seed-stitched highlights give the eyes their sparkle, whilst straight-stitched whiskers suggest an attitude all aquiver with curiosity.*
22.25 x 12.25cm (8¾ x 4¾in)

polypody (*Polypodium vulgare*) (Plate 38) is an excellent practice subject – worked this way the leaves should be no more difficult than the broad foliage of the greater periwinkle (*Vinca major*).

In contrast to the essential establishment of the correct angle of stitching on leaves and flowers to create a realistic effect, the fairy is so loosely worked as to be almost undefined. Only her wings fall back to a pivot point in long radial stitches. Her body is given minimal outline: flesh tones, hair and facial features are all suggested by the tiniest of speckled seed stitches, in turn diffusing into an aura of pink specks in fine cellophane thread. This 'now-you-see-it, now-you-don't' effect is surely in the very nature of the other realm.

The stoat in Plate 39 is an altogether more worldly character. Almost half of the carnivorous animals in Europe belong to the weasel family (*Mustelidae*), from the tiny weasel itself to the otter, badger and polecat, but the stoat (*Mustela erminea*), slim and savage yet endearingly playful and attractive, is one of the most successful. The stoat has few natural predators – humankind has been its greatest enemy. Persecuted by gamekeepers and depleted by the knock-on effects of myxomatosis on its favourite prey of rabbits, the stoat was once also hunted widely for its fur, or more precisely its tail, for cloaks and regalia bordered with ermine (the stoat's white winter coat, its tail tipped with black) were once the passion of the aristocracy. In high summer, though, at least that threat was in abeyance.

Seen full-faced, it is easy to establish the core or growing point of any subject (see Fig 28) – here the stoat's delicate pink nose. Work the integral facial features first, then gradually begin to build up the strata of radial *opus plumarium* falling back towards the core. The sinuous S-shaped contours of the body are the perfect vehicle for this technique. To contrast the dense working of the primary subject in this study I have chosen light, flyaway companion effects in the shape of the long, delicate grasses and the dandelion clock.

In high summer, grasses are flowering profusely. The medievals called June the 'hay-month' and modern sufferers from hay fever are well aware when the grass pollen begins to fly! We tend to think of grass as green but at this time of the year it is suffused with other shades as mauve, pink and purple spikelets form protective sheaths that surround the petal-less flowers. Decorative grasses are some of the simplest yet most effective ways to add interest to a study. In Plate 38 I have created a slightly stylized sheep's-fescue (*Festuca ovina*) with snake stitch, stem stitch and short wedges of radial work tipped with long straight stitches in silver (see Fig 29).

Wildflower meads – unspoilt, mixed grazing pastures – are rare nowadays. Modern farming methods have produced richer fields of finely cultivated, nutritious grass but something has been lost along the way. On an early summer morning, with the dew still glistening, what we

Fig 27 *The common polypody (like other ferns) is related to the horsetail, an ancient form of plant life that once dominated the whole planet. The deeply serrated leaves (top) need special attention: imagine the leaf whole by sketching a simple foliate contour around the more complicated outline (middle). Suggest the directional flow of* opus plumarium *across the whole field (bottom, upper half) and extrapolate this angle of stitching within the contours of the fern itself (lower half).*

Fig 28 *Like most animals, the core of stitching for members of the* mustelidae *family is at the nose. The nose itself (see also Plate 42) should be worked, possibly in a contrasting texture, in perpendicular straight stitching, in this case creating a broad core. The otter's luxurious coat can then be built up stratum by stratum, each feeding into the next, as with the stoat in Plate 39.*

think of today as weeds become magical: the spherical clocks of the dandelion scattered atop the grasses hover like pearls stitched randomly on to rich green velvet. The basic method of working the tiny dandelion (*Taraxacum officinale*) 'parachutes' can be better seen on its cousin, the goat's beard (*Tragopogon pratensis*) (Plate 40).

Generations of children have 'told the time' by blowing away the down of the dandelion 'clock', and have picked the flowers only to find they immediately and frustratingly close up when brought indoors, or in dull weather. The goat's beard goes one step further, closing its flower at midday – a characteristic that gives it its other country name, 'Jack-go-to-bed-at-noon'. Against a black background the 'sunburst' outline of the parachutes creates a firework effect, highlighted by a tiny seed stitch in metallic silver at each core. Both the dandelion and the goat's-beard clocks are worked in as fine a thread as possible and, unlike the area *within* the outline of the fern's leaf, are stitched directly on to the background fabric without a distinct, transferred outline. Any outline that was transferred might be too thick to be covered by a single strand of silk. Suggest the outer extremity of the feature with a few light dots, the inner core of each 'sunburst' similarly and allow the subject to build up gradually around those few basic essentials (see Fig 30).

The corn cockle (*Agrostemma githago*), also in Plate 40, is another wildflower of arable land that is becoming increasingly rare. Its elongated, teardrop-shaped buds are similar in outline to those of the goat's beard and need to be approached carefully if the correct directional stitching

'don't be afraid to add a few touches of artistic licence'

Fig 29 (1) By analyzing the curve of the design, the correct directional sweep of the snake stitch used for both the grass blades and the stem of the dandelion is easily achieved. (2) Grass seeds are worked in small lozenges of radial opus plumarium *with long straight stitches to describe their 'whiskers'. (3) The small details of the goat's beard are not transferred on to the fabric. Small dots (a) suggest the positioning of inner sunbursts of straight radial stitches (b), overlaid by a finer thread that completes the clock (c). A silver seed stitch at the centre of each sunburst lifts the finished motif.*

Plate 40 (opposite) Whilst green is certainly the optimal shade of summer, it is often the colour most difficult to quantify – in June, in particular, there seem to be an infinite combination of hues to explore. From yellow and gold-greens to pinkish beige and blue-greens, the choice appears inexhaustible. Choose your palette of threads methodically: whenever you acquire a new colour, try to find one lighter and one darker thread within the same 'family' of shades. Remember, too, that if you are using a fine enough gauge you can mix shades together in the needle, just as a painter mixes watercolours or oils. 21 x 13.5cm (8¼ x 5¼in)

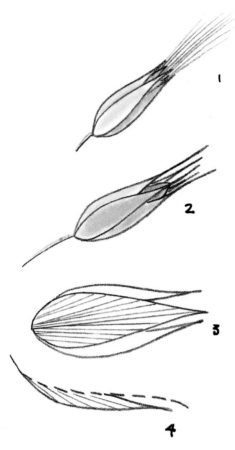

Fig 30 *(1 and 2) The closed head of the mature goat's beard and the bud of the corn cockle present similar contours. (3) The elongated lozenges can be approached similarly to the seeds in Fig 27 with radial work converging upon the basal core. (4) Peripheral half-lozenges should be worked in directional* opus plumarium *falling back to a (hidden) elongated core behind the foreground sepal.*

is to be achieved (Fig 30). On its flower, a few seed stitches in gold metallic thread have been incorporated at the core. These are echoed in the legs of the bumblebee. The pollen sac is yellow, drawing the eye around the simple design. Don't be afraid to add a few touches of artistic licence to even the most accurate of botanical studies to give an extra 'lift' to a design. Gold in particular is the colour of the sun and what could be more appropriate to a midsummer project?

I have interpreted the summer solstice, the longest day and the shortest night, which now falls on 21 June, in Plate 41 in the style of 8th-century Anglo-Saxon embroidery using plenty of gold thread. A stylized golden horse is resplendent beneath a spiralling gold sun, both worked in surface-couched passing thread. The jigsaw of colour patterned around them is worked in split stitch in colours that would once have been produced from natural hedgerow dyes such as woad, madder and saffron. Horses and the sun have always had a special connection. In many mythologies the chariot of the sun is drawn across the heavens by splendid horses and this little icon-like study is one of a set in this book suggesting the traditional festivals of spring and autumn equinox, summer and winter solstice (see also Plate 23 page 35, Plate 68 page 105 and Plate 80 page 123).

The joys of high summer are manyfold, and whilst the shifting of the ancient calendar has meant that the astronomical 'dog-days' of summer (when the dog star, Sirius, is at its highest) fall strictly speaking within July, many country folk have always associated them with those long hot days when dog roses have blown about the hedges 'unkempt . . . an English unofficial rose' ('The Old Vicarage, Granchester' Rupert Brooke).

For those fortunate enough to have a dog of their own it is also the best time of the year for 'walkies'! The overpowering heat of late summer is still to come, the rainy days of spring passed, and who can resist those bright, eager 'what's-keeping-you?' eyes (Plate 42). Animal portraits, especially those of much-

'I find it best to work from good photographs – and if possible to have a personal encounter with the sitter!'

Plate 41 *Whilst much early Anglo-Saxon*
secular embroidery appears at first glance to
be abstract, there is rarely a complete absence
of thematic or symbolic content. Zoomorphs –
apparently unidentifiable, often scrolling beasts
(see also Fig 58, page 123) – can usually be
traced to some recognizable animal, in this case
a prancing horse, front foot raised to paw the
ground, phallus and tail interwoven.
6.5 x 5.25cm (2½ x 2in)

loved pets, are amongst the most difficult subject for the embroiderer. Not only do we need to adhere to all the usual rules of technique but interpretation and character must come through. I find it best to work from good photographs – and if possible to have a personal encounter with the sitter! If you are not confident enough to make a sketch from your photographs, good black-and-white photos lend themselves well to being traced – use a light box if you have one, or lean your photo and tracing paper lightly against a window with bright sunlight flooding in. Pay particular attention to the eyes (opening them up a little more than the original) and use bold changes of shade to accentuate facial contours such as the muzzle, stop and brows. Basically, the rule of working toward the growing point holds true for all dogs – in this case a lovely wet nose!

In late June a warm walk in the wild woods is a perfect precursor to the long hot season to come – or a cool green suggestion of the moist, velvety depths of a more typical English summer.

Plate 42 *Tess, a much-loved springer spaniel, is the subject of this portrait. In fairly large-scale animal studies it is important to effect an obvious change in texture between the shiny, smooth waves of the coat and the matt areas of nose and tongue. Contrasting floss silk with stranded cotton begins the transformation but equally important is the type and direction of the stitching. On the latter features, straighter less flexible work allows abrupt transitions between light and shade – whilst the old trick of a couple of white seed stitches suggest a shiny highlight on the healthily damp nose.*
11 x 11.5cm (4¼ x 4½in)

HELEN M.
STEVENS

JULY

July is the first of the modern months to be named after a real person. Julius Caesar was, 'from his mother's womb untimely ripped' ('Macbeth', Act V, Scene VIII) in this month. We still commemorate this event despite the rather more attractive Anglo-Saxon 'moed monath' or 'mead month', named for the flowery meadows then in bloom that gave rise to the potent alcoholic mead of many a grand pagan celebration.

High summer has arrived: everything is vivid and multichrome. Flowers burst into life with a passion, live for a single day and give way to their successors, as tall spikes of blooms, broad fronds of foliage and dense, interwoven tapestries of stems conspire to take over hedgerow and garden border alike. No two days are similar; petals fall each long summer evening, only to be replaced the following morning. Nights are warm and starlit – the perfect time for late barbecues, patriotic firework displays and, for hard-pressed nature, a time to rest and recuperate from the exertions of early summer.

Truthfully, few of us feel like stitching during a long hot summer, but now is the time to absorb atmosphere, make sketches and think ahead. Soak up colour, make notes, maybe even press a few flowers into the leaves of a favourite book (using tissue paper to protect the pages) ready for later reference. Red-hot ruby is the colour, and gemstone, of July (Plate 43, left). Cool blues and mauves reflect the month's traditionally associated flowers, the larkspur and mallow.

LIBERTY, EQUALITY
AND THE COLOUR PURPLE

'A real live nephew of my Uncle Sam,
Born on the Fourth of July . . .'
('Yankee Doodle Dandy' George M. Cohan)

Fig 31 Three very different members of the Malvaceae family: clockwise from the top, the hibiscus, common mallow (Plate 45) and hollyhock (Plate 43). All three have pollen-bearing organs that look like little clusters of tiny seeds and, indeed, are best worked in small seed stitches that describe their texture perfectly.

As a child, I spent some of my most formative years in the United States, and can still recall the excitement that came with the arrival of July: just a few more days of preparation to go before Independence Day picnics, barbecues, parades and fireworks.

It is, of course, pure coincidence that 4 July is Midsummer's Eve by the old Julian calendar, but country folk emigrating to North America in the 18th century may well have influenced certain elements of the celebration by taking their own traditions into the New World. In a number of English towns until quite recently there was an emphasis on eating outdoors and parading through the streets in decorated carts on this date, and other ancient folk customs and songs certainly crossed the Atlantic well before Independence – the traditional song the 'Cutty Wren' (little wren) was recorded as early as 1744.

Plate 43 shows the tiny Jenny wren (*Troglodytes troglodytes*) in that most vibrant and prolific of July's garden flowers, the hollyhock. Wrens are much beloved in folklore – always the embodiment of the female, just as the robin was the male. Both were regarded as sacred birds, not to

'high summer has arrived: everything is vivid and multichrome'

Plate 43 (page 66) John Gerard's Historie of Plantes, more usually called 'Gerard's Herbal', refers to the hollyhock as the 'Outlandish Rose' – a gorgeous name for a gorgeous plant. With most of the medicinal applications of its wild cousins, the mallows, and with such outstanding beauty it is small wonder that hollyhocks became popular centuries ago in cottage, formal and herb gardens alike. In this apparently simply study thought has been given to depicting the flowers from a variety of angles to explore all their aspects.
Embroidery shown life-size 25.5 x 17.25cm (10 x 7in)

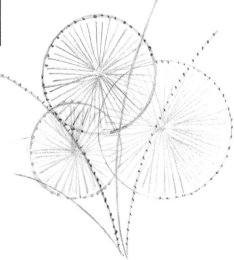

Plate 44

'. . . and you know your fate is, where the Empire State is, all you contemplate is, the view from Miss Liberty's dome . . .' ('It's Nice to go Travelling' Cahn/Van Heusen). The Statue of Liberty has been part of American popular culture since it was first built. This type of embroidery should be hung in a location where it will benefit from good artificial light – a spotlight from one side or an overhead picture strip light would be perfect. Tones and textures are subtle, so they need display emphasis.
21 x 12cm ($8^1/_4$ x $4^3/_4$in)

Fig 32 Remember the last firework display you enjoyed? Have some fun roughing out the circles and arcs of the bursting pyrotechnics before you commit them to transfer, then only trace off a suggestion of the spectacle to come – an outer ring of dots for the sunbursts and a hatched line for the arching rockets. Work out a colour theme in advance and plan where the shades will overlap, then let your seed stitches intermingle as the fireworks burst simultaneously. 'Light the blue touch paper and stand well back . . .'

be harmed or have their eggs taken for fear of ill luck befalling the thief. 'The Robin Redbreast and the Wren are God Almighty's cock and hen', warned an old saying. Despite its dull colouring, the wren has quite complicated markings. Browns and greys graduate irregularly from head to tail and detailed bars and speckles are most easily described by overlaid ticking or studding.

Hollyhocks have a long history of cultivation dating back over 500 years. They were thought to have originated in China, like their relative *Hibiscus rosa-sinensis* (Fig 31) though recently a Mediterranean pedigree has emerged.

'colours are picked up and emphasized by a window mount in a similar shade'

However, regardless of where they first flowered, they are the fireworks of the herbaceous border and have always reminded me of bright bursting rockets, towering above their neighbours. Simple radial *opus plumarium* falling back to a seed-stitched core of pollen describes the open flowers, whilst directional work is perfect for the centrally veined leaves.

With the beauty of nature so relatively simple to capture in embroidery, it can be tempting to avoid more challenging subjects but there is something exciting about stretching the imagination into new dimensions and fireworks are just such a challenge (Plate 44). Light and movement (in particular the latter) are, of course, essential elements in the spectacle of a firework display – but how can this be suggested in embroidery? Simplicity and an implied synchronicity can be a solution. Working entirely in seed stitches in metallic and blending filaments, the soaring sweep of rockets and the sunburst of spherically exploding fireworks overlap and intermingle with each other, colours blending as with the red, white and blue of the three uppermost shapes (Fig 32).

The Statue of Liberty is as potent a symbol of the USA as the flag itself. It was given to the American Republic by the French nation (who celebrate Bastille Day later in the month on 14 July) to commemorate the Centenary of Independence in 1876. It was ten years in the building and finally unveiled a decade later. Here, it is treated stylistically, with fine twisted silk threads used in straight stitch for both the statue and plinth, voided and highlighted to suggest, in turn, both deep shadow and the reflections of the fireworks. Only the flame in the uplifted torch is worked in floss silk.

Taking a single colour as a recurrent theme can also stimulate an interesting exploration of ideas (see Plates 45, 46, 47 and 48). One gloriously warm July evening I was at a party and out on the moonlit lawn music wafted from the French windows. 'And now the purple dusk of twilight time steals across the meadows of my heart, high up in the sky the little stars climb . . .' ('Stardust' Carmichael/Parish). The deep purples, mauves and pinks of a hot summer night seemed to invite interpretation: Plate 45 is a minimalist approach.

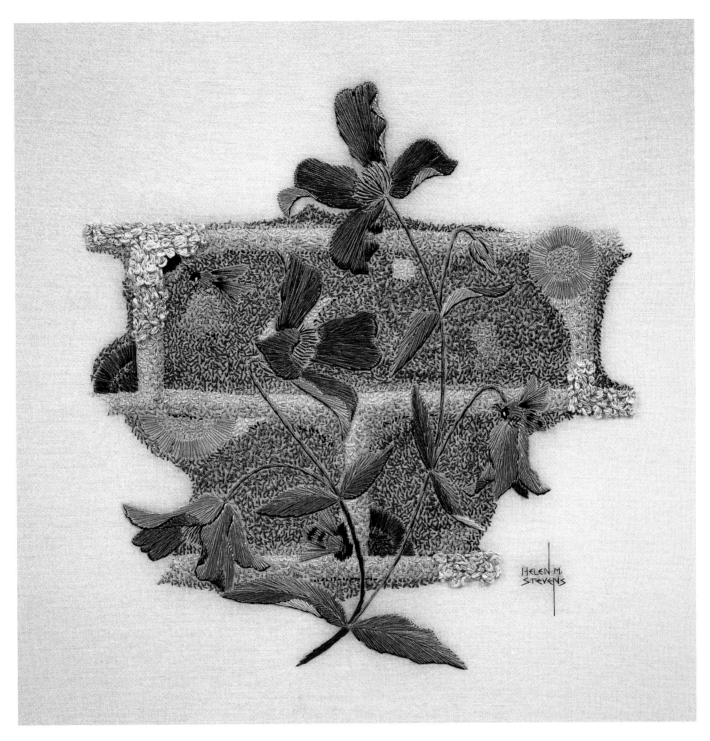

Plate 46 *The flower of the clematis consists of four beautifully coloured sepals – petals are entirely absent. When the sepals fall, the thick mass of stamens at the centre of the flower (here worked in fine shadow-lined stem stitch) enlarge to become feathery clusters (the 'traveller's joy' of the hedgerow are the fluffy seed heads of the wild clematis). See Plates 62 and 63 on pages 95 and 96, and Fig 45 on page 94.*
15.25 x 15.25cm (6 x 6in)

The common mallow (*Malva sylvestris*) in Plate 45 is a country cousin of the stately hollyhock and exotic hibiscus. It is a familiar hedgerow flower which runs riot every summer. Its attractive rose-purple flower is shown here without the complication of leaves, in company with the purple hairstreak butterfly (*Quercusia quercus*), whilst a suggestion of early evening is created by the application of tiny sequins in indigo, mauve and silver-lilac, caught down by clear cellophane thread. The colours are picked up and emphasized by a window mount in a similar shade. A very different effect can be created by making a feature of the background of the study.

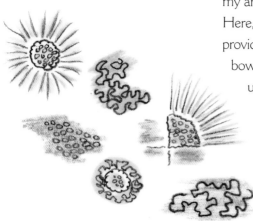

Fig 33 *The extraordinary shapes and textures of lichen are like a firework display in miniature. Study an old, weathered, slightly crusty brick wall: where moulds and lichens have taken hold, the surface will have slightly fractured sunbursts, corollas and meandering zigzags of fibre creating fascinating patterns. Sketch them into your pocket notepad to resurrect back at your drawing board. This is the time to get out some of those 'I-knew-they'd-come-in-handy' specialist threads.*

'Beside a garden wall, when stars are bright, you are in my arms . . .' ('Stardust' Carmichael/Parish) (Plate 46). Here, an old red-brick wall, dotted with lichens and moss, provides a backdrop for the clematis (*Clematis viticella*) or bower vine. The clematis is embroidered first, using the usual principles for floral stitching (see *Helen M. Stevens' Embroidered Flowers*, D&C, 2000). Then, working once again in that most versatile yet simple of stitches, seed stitch, the main areas of the bricks together with the intervening mortar, is built up in russet shades using a single strand of stranded cotton and creamy ecru twisted silks. Textural features, such as lichen, are added in surface-couched bouclé silk or straight and seed-stitched floss silk (see Fig 33). Mason bees (*Osmia rufa*) buzz between the flowers, their deeply excavated tunnels suggested by a dense working of black matt thread.

Even the best photographic reference books on butterflies find it difficult to recreate the colour purple. The wings of blue and mauve butterflies have iridescent colours: caused by sunlight diffracting off tiny corrugations on the surface of the wing scales, all colours

Plate 47 *The decline in the number of purple emperors is more likely due to a lack of its natural habitat (undisturbed woodland) than to persecution by butterfly hunters, although the Victorians went to great lengths to capture these prize beauties. If you are determined to see them in the flesh they can be tempted on to the woodland floor with rotting meat. For embroiderers' purposes, however, a good textbook with painted illustrations rather than photographs is the best reference material.*
8.25 x 8.25cm (3^1/$_4$ x 3^1/$_4$in)

Plate 48
'Mirrored colours, mystic gleams,
Fairy dreams . . .
Ah, the dog rose trembling over.'
('Butterflies' Alfred Noyes)
10.75 x 8.25cm (4¼ x 3¼in)

of the spectrum except blues are absorbed (see *Helen M. Stevens' Embroidered Butterflies*, D&C 2001). Purple, as every child knows, is a mixture of blue and red, and so to capture in photography a naturally occurring purple of this origin is almost impossible. How lucky, therefore, that we embroiderers are able to do so – effecting not only the shade but also the sheen and texture of the original.

The purple emperor (*Apatura iris*) (Plate 47) is one of England's loveliest, and sadly, now rarer butterflies. Like the purple hairstreak (Plate 45) it is attracted to the canopies of oak woodland and so is rarely seen at lower levels: flowers that scramble up to find light are likely to be one of its main floral stops. Morning glories (*Calystegia sepium*) stay open all night if there is a moon, and at dawn can be the first port of call for many butterflies. The wings of the purple emperor call for a mixture of Dalmatian dog spotting and radial *opus plumarium*. Work the spots first, including the elongated bar of white that stretches across both upper and lower wings (see Fig 34), then flood the radial work around them. Finally, work the outer strata of gold.

Fig 34 *The purple emperor butterfly is a perfect example of Dalmatian dog technique. Work the spots first, whether they be round, arched or elongated into bands (1) and then flood the radial* opus plumarium *around them (2).*

Liberty, equality and the colour purple - July 73

*'the complicated marking
of the swallowtail's wings are worked
entirely in Dalmatian dog spotting'*

'The nightingale sings his fairy tale, of paradise where roses grew . . .' ('Stardust' Carmichael/Parish). Another predominantly purple butterfly that is now rarely seen is the swallowtail (*Papilio machaon*) (Plate 48), and certainly not likely to be found with wild roses – but this is a fairy tale. Deep purple on black might seem like an equally unlikely combination but its richness, offset by the fresh creamy-yellow of the swallowtail's other shades and the delicate

Plate 49 *Bindweed can grow to vast heights, given an appropriate support. Several telegraphs poles in my village are swamped but the bright green foliage and white or pink flowers make such a pretty show that they are usually left throughout the summer. The deep-red throat of the swallow is rarely noticed in flight as they move so quickly but at rest is seen to best advantage. The marking has a distinct outline and the red strata of stitching should be terminated accurately. As with the blue-black of the lower throat into the creamy breast, there is no 'bleeding' of colours one into the next.*
16.5 x 10cm (6½ x 4in)

pink of the rose, makes a delicious fantasy. The complicated marking of the swallowtail's wings are worked entirely in Dalmatian dog spotting. Spots, of course, need not be round (as demonstrated in the bar on the purple emperor in Plate 47) and here they are mostly chevron shaped. The flooded radial work to the outer edges of the wings is fine, but in principle is worked in exactly the same manner as any broader expanse. The distinctive veins on the lower wings are worked in fine stem stitch into a void previously left.

The swallowtail takes its name, naturally, from its relatively long, forked tail's similarity to that of the swallow (*Hirundo rustica*). No bird is more redolent of summer than the swallow; its glossy blue-black plumage, high-pitched call in flight and pleasant twittering warble at rest are the very essence of the season. Every country person knows that when the swallows fly high the weather will be fine; when they fly low rain may well be on the way. This is based on sound logic and observation. In fair weather, air pressure is high and the flying insects that are the birds' staple diet (Plate 49) are in the upper air; when air pressure falls (as it does when rain approaches) the insects fly lower, and the swallows follow suit. Tiny lazy daisy stitches and a few straight legs are all that are needed to suggest these little 'motes' of life, the finer the thread the better (Fig 35). In this study, the swallow's high-wire perch is created by the couching of a thick gold cord. By whipping the ends of the cord down very firmly they flatten just at the point where the bird's feet grip hold of the branch to create a lifelike effect.

High summer has been a time of relative rest and recuperation for inhabitants of the natural world and entertainment for others, but the midsummer revels and self-congratulatory celebrations must soon come to an end. With August will come the first of the harvests, for many birds and animals further broods of youngsters and even the beginning of autumn's busy hoarding of food for the seasons to come.

Fig 35 Perspective is a strange animal. Because we know that gnats are much smaller than swallows, by working them at a larger scale (top right) we immediately suggest that they are in the foreground and the swallows are at a greater distance. By dotting in gnats in proportion to the birds (left and centre) we can trick the eye into believing that this is a really three-dimensional study. It is the same trick as working a few straight-stitched grasses at the foot of the framing features of a landscape (see Plate 36, pages 54/55 and Plate 74, pages 114/115). Don't be afraid to play with special effects.

'no bird is more redolent of summer than the swallow; its glossy blue-black plumage and high-pitched call in flight the very essence of the season'

AUGUST

August, like July, takes its name from a historical character, the Emperor Augustus (originally known as Octavius) who was Julius Caesar's grand-nephew. The eighth month was his as it coincided with all the good fortune of his reign: he was elected Consul, ended his wars and conquered Egypt. A problem arose when it was realized that August had only 30 days and July 31 – might the great Augustus be jealous? The Romans solved this knotty problem by borrowing a day from September and adding it on to August!

In Christian Europe, the eighth month marked the beginning of the harvest. 'Lammas', 1 August, may have taken its name from the traditional gifting of fat lambs to the Church (lamb-mass) as recognition of the fruits of the harvest to come, though it is possibly a corruption of the feast of Lugnas, an important Celtic god whose festival also marked the beginning of harvest. Certainly the gold and green of the harvest home are at their most mellow now. Though modern farming methods have brought the harvest forward, it is still during August that we begin to feel the deep stirrings of late summer: flaxen, silken, satin – the ripe fields ripple to the movement of a thousand tiny feet (Plate 50, left).

It is hard to escape from the allure of precious metals now. Gold seems to be everywhere – in the sun, the harvest, the shimmering wings of insects (Plate 54), even the warm masonry of historic buildings (Plate 55). Red and gold together suggest the richness of the season, royal blue adding to the pageantry. Sardonyx, the gold-red banded stone of mythology is August's gem, whilst poppies are the traditional flowers of this long, hot month.

SUMMER SPORTS

'I ripped my shirt and I teared my skin,
To bring the Master's harvest in.' (Traditional rhyme)

Delving deep into history it is possible to find some strange and almost sinister aspects to Lammas-tide and late summer revels. The ancient pagan tradition of sacrificing the summer 'king' may have been re-enacted as late as 1100 when the English king, William Rufus, was apparently murdered in the New Forest on 2 August. In many early harvest fairs, the 'Queen of Revels' is still an unconscious incarnation of the goddess whose murder of her husband-lover-child ensures the continuing regeneration of the earth. In a good year, the abundance of both natural and cultivated produce lends a feeling of decadent well-being to this most sensual time of the year.

Even the tiny pygmy shrew (*Sorex minutus*) (Plate 50), whose entire life is devoted to the frenetic hunt for food, finds its search less onerous at this season. The pygmy shrew is close to the limit at which a warm-blooded mammal can exist – any smaller and it would lose body heat so quickly that it would be unable to survive. As it is, if it fails to eat for more than two hours it will starve to death. Tiny insects, soil creatures (worms, slugs and snails) and insect larvae make up the bulk of its diet. Litters born early in the year may well be producing young of their own by July, the new generation of mothers taking their broods out 'crocodile fashion' to learn hunting skills in early August.

*Fig 36 The stag beetle (*Lucanus cervus*) is Britain's largest beetle, and at around 5cm (2in) long, it would be a brave shrew who attempted this adversary! Like mayfly (Plate 53), the adult lives only a short time after its emergence from pupal form. In the Middle Ages it was believed that the male stag beetle could (and would, if encouraged by witchcraft) fly with a red-hot coal in its jaws and set alight the houses of the unwary.*

'the gold and green of the harvest home are at their most mellow now'

Plate 50 (page 76) For all the world like children on a school outing, young shrews make their first foray out of the nest: single file, they have been seen forming a 'daisy chain', each holding the former's tail in its mouth. Against a black background, shadow lining is, of course, unnecessary, but void carefully to differentiate between specific features and planes. The golden whiskers of the corn are reflected by the use of a couched gold thread to highlight the coil of the snail's shell. Don't be afraid to use little 'tricks' to lead the eye from one feature to the next. Embroidery shown life-size 26.75 x 19.75cm (10½ x 7¾in)

Plate 51 *If you are fortunate enough to live in an arable farming area, you may well have harvest mice as neighbours, though you will rarely catch a glimpse. The best way to observe them is to stroll along the headland of a ripe field, find a secluded spot and sit quietly until dusk. Any time between May and October (though August is the height of the breeding season) you may hear the 'chicka-chicka-chicka' of a male in pursuit of his lady-love. You may also hear the shriek of disapproval as she declines his advances. If you are lucky the resulting rustle in the long grass will afford you a sight of the couple.*
15.25 x 11.5cm (6¼ x 4¼in)

The pygmy shrew, at around 6.4cm (2½in) long, head and body, is not much bigger than a stag beetle (Fig 36) and is a challenging subject for *opus plumarium*. The head of the mother shrew in Plate 50 (page 76) is worked in five strata, a void left between head and body, which is then worked in four strata. On a larger animal, extensive swathes of radial work would describe detailed contours but here a few short strata must do the work for us. Establish the flow of the stitches, as ever, radiating from the growing point and keep each strata to an appropriate width. Soften voids with a few feathering stitches in a finer strand.

Above the shrews, the vibrant colours of late summer flowers make a showy splash. Poppies (*Papaver rhoeas*) are still a common feature of arable

fields but the glorious blue of the cornflower (*Centaurea cynas*) is now rarely seen – 'improved' farming methods have reduced it to a garden escapee. It is a complex bloom of inner and outer florets that need to be sketched and worked in stages in order to produce an effective description (see Fig 37). The scentless mayweed (*Tripleurospermum inodorum*) is another once common flower of the cornfield, shown in Plate 51 with the delightful harvest mouse.

As its Latin name implies, the harvest mouse (*Micromys minutus*) vies with the pygmy shrew for the title of smallest rodent: its tail, at 6.4cm ($2^{1}/_{2}$in), doubles its overall length making it longer than its rival, but during August's peak breeding season, newly emerged young are, indeed, minute. At only 16 days old they become independent, leaving carefully woven nests to establish their own territory. Again, modern farming has made their traditional homes in cornfields less than ideal, but another aspect of 20th-century evolution has been to their benefit: the large undisturbed tracts of grassland at the verges and embankments of motorways have proved an ideal, if less picturesque, substitute.

As in Plate 50, the careful use of radial *opus plumarium* in finely contoured strata is the key to working the harvest mouse successfully. Seen full faced, the sweep of stitches towards the growing point is easily identifiable, stitches flowing around secondary cores at the forelegs, then progressing smoothly across tummy and haunches towards the little gripping toes. Feet and tail are worked in stranded cotton to contrast with the floss silk of the animals' fur. The prehensile tail is an excellent example of snake stitching, as are the coiling, reflexing blades of foliage.

'remember that your primary subjects will have a bearing upon the other elements of the study'

If we look at a similar subject in more detail (Plate 52) we can pick out the various elements that make these studies so appealing. Walt Disney discovered early in his feature animations that character was all important in his interpretations. We have discussed in earlier chapters the necessity to focus a subject's eyes and attention upon a

Fig 37 *Left: the beautiful cornflower is quite a complex bloom. Top right: work the florets in delicate* opus plumarium *in pale and dark blue for inner and outer surfaces respectively. Middle right: work a corolla of radial* opus plumarium *in purple. Bottom: overlay seed stitches in dark blue and gold metallic threads to suggest the smaller elements at the flower's core.*

particular point. In Plate 50, each animal is engaged by a specific element of the design; in Plate 51 the harvest mouse looks directly at the viewer, whilst in Plate 52 he concentrates on the spider and web. This sets in motion the 'story' of the picture and leaves us free to concentrate on the ancillary features.

Remember that your primary subjects (the harvest mice in Plates 51 and 52) will have a bearing upon the other elements of the study. Their weight (minimal though it is) will affect the supporting features. A precarious balancing act on the corn stalk in Plate 51 bends the stem significantly; the more secure acrobatics in Plate 52 produce a lesser effect, but still the ear of corn inclines with the presence of its visitor. Frame your primary subjects with your secondary. The protective, encircling 'arm' of the leaf in Plate 51 cocoons the mouse; the bolder fellow in Plate 52 thrusts himself between ear and leaf to reach his goal.

In August, the insect world takes on an urgent burst of activity. Butterflies continue their laid-back enjoyment of the late summer but other insects begin their countdown to autumn. While flowers are still there to be enjoyed, full advantage must be taken. St Bartholomew's Day is on 24 August and he is, among other things, the patron saint of bee-keepers, honey-makers and mead-brewers. The willowherbs are a fine source of nectar – see Plates 53 and 54.

Great willowherb (*Epilobium hirsutum*) revels in some delicious country names: codlins-and-cream (codlins are cooking apples), apple-pie and cherry-pie plants. Crushed flowers and leaves certainly give off a fruity aroma but it has also been suggested that 'codlin' may be a corruption of 'codpiece', the fashionable Tudor accessory that protected the male member. A cursory examination of the fruiting body that succeeds the flower (see Fig 38 overleaf and October, Plate 63, page 96) requires no further explanation!

Simple radial work is ideal for the flower of the great willowherb, directional work for the leaves and stem stitch for the stem. Couple this with the radial and straight stitching required for the elephant hawkmoth (*Deilephila elpenor*) (Plate 53) and a delightful study can be created with the simplest of techniques. I always leave

Plate 52 *'Captain Courageous' was the name given to a feisty little mouse who regularly appeared at one of my student's windows, demanding titbits. The name was immediately transferred to this little fellow who has become my model for mouse portraiture.*
19 x 7cm (7^1/$_2$ x 2^3/$_4$in)

Plate 53 *Some species of mayfly (see May, Plates 30 and 31, pages 46 and 49) fly late into the summer and are often seen skimming the flowers of the great willowherb, which also enjoys a watery setting. Pale gold, green and silver, it creates a delicate counterbalance to the more extraordinary colours of the elephant hawkmoth – so called because its caterpillar resembles the trunk of an elephant, or so early entomologists thought!*
10.75 x 8.25cm (4^1/$_4$ x 3^1/$_4$in)

'I always leave a stand of wild willowherb in my garden to attract hawkmoths'

Fig 38 *The delicate bloom of the great willowherb gives way to a rather more indelicate fruiting body in the shape of a long 'codpiece' (right), the subject of much medieval and Tudor jest. These later produce 'old-man's beard' (see October, Plate 63, page 96 and Fig 48, page 99).*

a stand of wild willowherb in my garden to attract hawkmoths and in the autumn they become a marvellous tangle of 'old-man's beard' (see October Plate 63, page 96). The elephant hawkmoth caterpillar feeds mostly at night but it can also be found sunning itself on flowers during the day.

The slightly showier flower of the rosebay willowherb is also a draw to insects (Plate 54). The botanical name *Epilobium angustifolium* gives away the main flowering period of this attractive plant. It is also called 'fireweed', as it thrives in areas cleared by wildfire and it was one of the first plants to brighten the blasted bombsites of London both during and after the bombing raids of World War II. The broad-bordered bee hawkmoth (*Hemaris fuciformis*) (top right) is just one of the insects that is attracted to its yellow-stamened flowers. Although the wings of this bee-mimicking moth look complicated, they are actually easy to interpret. Transfer the outline of the 'broad border' only (Fig 39, top) and work this in a disjointed strata of radial work in gold thread. Work the tracery of the wings in fine silk (middle) and then overlay the whole wing with spaced radial stitches in cellophane thread (bottom). The ladybird (*Coccinella 7-punctata*) is given its seven-spotted wing-case design by studding

Fig 39 The broad-bordered bee hawkmoth is a sweet subject. Top: work the body in straight stitching and the broad wing borders in disjointed strata of radial work. Middle: suggest the veins of the cellular wing structure with fine straight stitching in a single strand of silk. Bottom: complete the body by working two rows of laddering on the lower segment.

overlaid on the *opus plumarium* of the case, and the common copper butterfly (*Lycaena phlaeas*) is worked in three simple strata of orange and brown.

The anniversary of the beheading of St John the Baptist was supposedly 29 August and consequently is his saint's day. Another John to whom August augured ill-fortune was the English King John 'Lackland' (1167–1216). After a fiery sermon preached in August 1214 by Stephen Langton, Archbishop of Canterbury, the Barons met at Bury St Edmunds in Suffolk, England to draw up the proposals that would eventually form Magna Carta. Bury still remembers the event annually.

The mellow month of August is surely the loveliest in which to visit the medieval buildings of England. Ancient masonry glows with the warmth of late summer sun, whilst everywhere the sights and sounds of 'Olde Englande' conjure the charm of Albion, its ancient name. Plate 55 is a composite design to commemorate a birthday and was commissioned to reflect the aspects of a long and colourful life. The great Abbey Gate of Bury St Edmunds forms the centrepiece, whilst around it are grouped elements of family history and national heritage. A study of this kind is a wonderful heirloom to pass down to future generations, in this case bringing together emblems of school and regiment, home and away – and a passion for that most English of all sports, cricket. The magnificent gateway into the Abbey Gardens (the last remnant

*Plate 54 Lewis Carroll's creation, Alice (*Alice's Adventures in Wonderland*), commented to her friend the Gnat that the scientific names of most insects are of 'no use to them but are useful to the people who name them'. True, in that a seven-spotted ladybird can be identified as different to a twenty-four spotted ladybird without having to count each tiny spot each time. Similarly, it would be pedantic to try and use Dalmatian dog technique on such a minute subject – studding overlaid in black on the bright scarlet of the wing case will do the job just as well.*
10.75 x 10.25cm (4¼ x 4in)

Plate 55 *The badge of the Suffolk Regiment crowns this study, worked in metallic threads highlighted by floss silks and plied black and gold. It is a traditional and formalized use of embroidery to convey stylized subject matter. Slightly less rigid is the interpretation of the 'Minden' rose (centre right, called after the Battle of Minden, the Regiment's finest hour) and the Tudor-style rose (centre left, emblem of King Edward's Grammar School). Birds, flowers and foliage are worked naturalistically, and the cricket match with an impressionist flavour. Mix and match your styles of work in this type of sampler commemorative piece.*
28 x 20.5cm (11 x 8in)

Plate 56 *(detail of Plate 55) Like fireworks (July, Plate 44, page 69) a cricket match is not a subject that immediately recommends itself for embroidery, but that, surely, is the joy of such a challenge. Remember to pause at design stage and consider the techniques available to you. Sometimes, as here, a simplistic approach can be the most successful.*
Detail shown: 8.25 x 7cm (3¹/₄ x 2³/₄in)

Fig 40 *At a distance, detail is unnecessary. Learn to draw 'carrot' people. Sketch a carrot shape (top and top left), add a round head and then scribble in arms, legs, clothes and so on, as the spirit moves you. In the cricket match in Plate 56 (a detail of Plate 55) there is little colour – line and stitch direction suggests the movement and interaction of the characters.*

of the Abbey destroyed by Henry VIII) is worked in twisted silk straight stitching, keeping the emphasis on the perpendicular, overlaid in places to pick out details such as the portcullis and the stone moulding. This is a rigid, disciplined interpretation – the antithesis of the impressionist treatment of the cricket match (see the detail shown in Plate 56).

Reproduced here at approximately life-size, the 'sketchy' approach to the scene is clear. The principles of light and shade, shadow lining and perspective are followed, but there precision ends. Emphasis is on line and movement: just as in water-colour or pastel work a 'carrot' can become a person (see Fig 40), so in embroidery a few simple black and white stitches create a cricketer. Here, miniaturization meets improvization.

'the hedgerow shifts imperceptibly from green-gold to amber and red'

As summer draws to a close, new pastimes beckon. The hedgerow shifts imperceptibly from green-gold to amber and red. The breaks are applied as nature's traffic lights tell us to slow down, take stock and beware of the surprises still in store.

SEPTEMBER

With September and the coming of true autumn, the names of the months are increasingly confusing. This should by rights be the seventh month, although the various calendar alterations over the millennia have utterly confused any apparent logic. For the Romans, who's year began with March, this was an appropriate name, but the Anglo-Saxons simply called it 'gerst monath' – the month of the barley harvest.

It is now that fruits and berries begin to brighten the hedgerows: red, purple, blue-black hips, blackberries and sloes (Plate 57, left) cling to their late-leafing boughs, whilst apples, other fruits and leaves begin to fall. The former ferment into an alcoholic treat for birds and insects alike, the latter create a patchwork of vibrant, quilted effects, richly padded or starkly skeletonized in a crazy last-minute burst of colour. Michaelmas Eve, 28 September, was traditionally the last day on which to pick blackberries as it was thought that the Devil spat on them on St Michael's Day and turned them bitter.

With the autumn equinox comes the beginning of longer evenings and shorter days and the practicalities of embroidery are suddenly more alluring. Take advantage of shows and exhibitions to collect new threads and fabrics, check that your spotlight is efficient and plan for projects to come. Some of the ephemeral effects of autumn – early-morning frost on cobwebs, late-afternoon sunlight on fallen leaves, the last dance of insects around the traveller's joy, can be sketched (or even photographed) for later study. Cool sapphire, the colour of early frosts, is September's stone, whilst the aster represents the last of the season's flowers.

ALL THAT GLISTERS

'Try to remember the kind of September,
when love was an ember
about to billow . . .' ('The Fantasticks' Schmit/Jones)

'September, the perfect time for love . . .'
('The Fantasticks' Schmit/Jones) and there certainly is a mellowness to a fine September that speaks of warm, heady country wines, the rustle of the first-fallen leaves, the tang of autumnal bonfires – a rich, fruity atmosphere. The largest country fair in all England was once held regularly on 14 September, Holy Cross Day, at Stourbridge near Cambridge – three days of pleasure, sports and commercial profit.

Indeed, September was a time when profit could be had for free from the hedgerows (Plate 57). Until and during World War II, rose-hips were gathered and sold to manufacturers to produce rose-hip syrup, blackberries for jelly and jam and the fruit of the blackthorn for sloe gin (though this was more often produced at home by simply adding the sloes to pre-bought gin and allowing further fermentation, to virtually double the quantity and considerably increase the alcoholic content!).

Brambles, or blackberries (*Rubus fruticosus*), are a source of perplexity to many botanists. There are over 2,000 varieties or sub-species that look considerably different from one region to another. It is sound advice

Fig 41 As in Fig 28 (page 61), the sudden flash of movement and colour can often prompt an equally impromptu sketch. Always keep a few coloured pencils and a notepad within reach. A quick sketch such as this could evolve into a major study such as Plate 57.

Plate 57 (page 86) The white 'punctuation mark' on the underside of its lower wing gives the comma butterfly its name. Many handbooks suggest that the butterfly be identified by this mark but is it surely of secondary importance to the ragged, deeply indented contour of the wings themselves, quite unlike those of any other British butterfly. Its markings, too, are variable and diffuse. Whilst Dalmatian dog spotting is ideal for the easily defined black markings, the paler shadows may be more successfully suggested by overlaying long ticking stitches in rough chevrons. The comma, something of a maverick among butterflies, also requires rules to be broken in embroidery. Rules of perspective may also be bent – why should a bumblebee not wing-in head first, like the Lancaster bomber its droning buzz always suggests?
Embroidery shown life-size 25.5 x 17.75cm (10 x 7in)

Plate 58 The warm brown of the red admiral's inner wing pattern proves that a dull shade can still be attractive, even spectacular, in the appropriate place. Alongside the smart black and red of the rest of the butterfly's livery, it is more suggestive of a military than a naval uniform. Its name, however, is a corruption of red 'admirable', its original country nickname. Here, Dalmatian dog spotting creates the larger of the white markings (upper wings), the tiny spots added in studding. On the lower wings, blue chevrons and black spots are surrounded by flooded strata of brown and red.
10 x 8.25cm (4 x 3¹/₂in)

not to eat blackberries after Michaelmas – the culprit who 'spits' on them is actually the flesh-fly (*Sarcophaga carnaria*), whose dribbled saliva makes the fruit easier for the insect to ingest. The hip or fruit of the dog rose (*Rosa canina*), gives the lie to the epithet 'dog' being applied to plants whose produce is worthless as generations of children were brought up on its vitamin C-rich medicinal syrup (see also June, Plate 37, page 56). Blackthorn (*Prunus spinosa*) is thought to be the parent plant of all cultivated plums, useful enough in domestic terms but it is also the traditional wood from which the harvesters' hay-rakes were made.

'take advantage of shows and exhibitions to collect new threads and fabrics'

Late-flying butterflies such as the comma (*Polygonia c-album*) (Plate 57) and red admiral (*Vanessa atalanta*) (Plate 58) bring flashes of bright movement to the wayside, and now is a perfect time to watch them close up. Like birds, they find the fermenting fruits irresistible and become quite tipsy, resting, wings akimbo, in the sunshine of a warm afternoon. Sketch them in 'shorthand' to remind yourself later of their juxtaposition to fruits and flowers (Fig 41). Remember you can always go back to a good textbook to fill in the details later, before you transfer your designs on to fabric.

Blackberries are a delightful subject for embroidery. They are easily recreated by working the individual 'berry-lets' in straight stitching at random, in varying angles, massed together to form the whole berry. Then add tiny seed stitches between the segments to suggest the dusty detritus of the hedgerow and the 'bloom' of the berries themselves (see Fig 42). The same technique can be used for similar fruits, such as raspberries and mulberries. Blackberries and apples go together like apple pie and cream – and the red admiral is a devotee of both. William Wordsworth wrote in his poem 'To a Butterfly', 'this plot of orchard ground is ours', but naturally occurring apples are just as attractive to the insect – crab apples and brambles are often found together.

By September, the leaves of the bramble are beginning to degrade: dull green to ochre, gold to brown, they start their decline into autumnal oblivion. But even as they fade and fragment they become beautiful (Plate 59). Honeycomb stitch (as discussed in February, Plate 17 on page 24 and Fig 10 on page 25) can describe the skeletal architecture of a leaf as well as the cellular structure of a wing (see also December Plate 75, page 116). Runners, shot out of the plant's early summer growth, sustain trios or quintets of leaves that tenaciously hang on to their stems. Establish the flow of the *opus plumarium* on the outer edge of each leaf and then work spaced directional stitching towards the elongated cores formed by the vein. Honeycomb between the radial stitches, allowing the whole pattern to flow around the veins. Vary your colours to complement the un-degraded parts of the leaves.

'honeycomb stitch can describe the skeletal architecture of a leaf as well as the cellular structure of a wing'

Honeycomb stitch can be used in various ways to suggest a diversity of foliate effects. With the end of summer, plants whose beauty is less dependent on flowers and more on their leaves, come into ascendancy. Begonias are among the most attractive (Plate 60), and

Fig 42 Blackberries are among the most satisfying of berry subjects – they really do look juicy! A short section of rapidly graduating stem stitch creates the claw shape of the reflexing sepals (see Fig 21, page 48). Then work each 'berry-let' in massed straight stitches, keeping each section at a different angle to its neighbours (to catch and refract the light at equally differing angles), and finally add tiny seed stitches in pale green or grey randomly between the 'berry-lets'.

their texture as well as their vivid colouring begs interpretation in embroidery. Here, I have taken the experiment in Plate 17, page 24 – where a single colour has been allowed to dominate – a stage further. The glorious forms of *Begonia masoniana* (top) and *Begonia rex* (below) have first been worked in up to five strata of directional *opus plumarium* (Dalmatian dog spots incorporated in the outer strata of the latter) and then completely overlaid in honeycomb stitch worked, respectively, in a fine strand of silver and gold metallic thread. A quilted, almost padded, effect is achieved. The order of working is set out in Fig 43 overleaf.

'with the approach of the autumnal equinox, harvest is largely over'

With the approach of the autumnal equinox (spring equinox in the southern hemisphere) on 23 September, harvest was (and is) largely over. In days when the harvest was undertaken by hand, now was the time for gleaners to move into the fields and pick up what fallen grains they could to eke out their survival in the months to come. The 'corn dolly', an incarnation of the universal fertility goddess, was made from the last sheaf of corn to be harvested, to be kept safe until her time came for veneration at the turn of the winter/spring season. Time to take stock and celebrate.

In England, in Norfolk and Suffolk in particular, the last wagon of the harvest was known as the 'Horkey load' (names varied throughout the country: Holkey, Hocky and so on) and the day following was 'Drinking Day', a title that needs little explanation! From time immemorial, the end of harvest and the coming of the equinox were greeted similarly. Plate 61 shows an interpretation of the autumnal equinox in the Anglo-Saxon series already described (see also Plate 23 page 35, Plate 41 page 65 and Plate 80 page 123).

'many specialist "hobby" plants become the passion of their owners'

In Plate 61 a stag is shown below the sun/moon motif, surrounded by a jigsaw of split-stitched colours in traditional Anglo-Saxon style (see also Fig 44). Moonbeams and sunbeams radiate from the sun/moon motif, whilst a landscape is suggested by more horizontal split stitching in the lower half of the design, behind the stag.

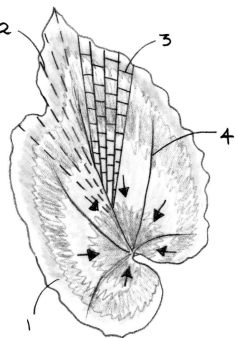

Fig 43 *The quilted effect of the begonia leaves is fun to work. (1) Radial* opus plumarium *falls back to the core in four (or more) strata of different colours. (2) Work straight directional stitches from the outer edge of the motif to the central vein, leaving this void for now. (3) Transform the straight directional stitches into honeycomb stitch (see Fig 10, page 25), in gold or silver thread. (4) Finally, couch the veins in metallic thread along the voids left by the* opus plumarium.

Plate 60 *A study such as this is more time consuming than the little fantasy in Plate 59 but the idea could nevertheless be adapted to make a personal statement. Many specialist 'hobby' plants become the passion of their owners – what better gift than an embroidery based on that enthusiasm? Leaves that could be treated in this way include the African violet and the auricula (March, Plate 21, page 32) – in fact any plant with a fleshy, succulent leaf would work well.*
10.25 x 11.5cm (4¼ x 4½in)

Plate 61 Anglo-Saxon embroidery was eclectic in design and stylized in execution but full of detail and vivacity. To recreate their relatively limited palette of colours – mainly based on plant dyes – we need to choose carefully. Red, blue (dark and light), green, yellow and beige silk, together with gold and silver metallic thread, produce an authentic effect. Metallic 'passing' thread, though technically able to be pulled through the fabric with a large enough needle, is better used surface couched in this instance. During the 8th century a thick gold or silver 'leaf' was hand cut into minute strips and wound around a horse's tail hair to produce such thread. Today's equivalent is machine made, usually with a silk core.
6.25 x 5cm (2¹/₂ x 2in)

Deer have always been important symbols at this time of the year: for most species their antlers are now fully formed in readiness for the rutting season ahead. This is the time when Herne the Hunter appears to the unwary lost in autumnal woodland, the Gabriel Hounds (St Michael shares his saint's day with Gabriel) and the Wild Hunt are to be most feared. Not surprisingly, therefore, the 'traveller's joy' so named by John Gerard in his Herbal of 1597, was sought for its 'goodly shadow whiche they make with their thick bushing and clymbing' – a protection from the night-stalking demons of the woodland.

Explored in its cultivated version in Plate 46 (July, page 71) the clematis is a plant of exquisite diversity. In high summer its sepals (in garden varieties at least) enjoy a long flowering season, adding colour to the most arid corner, and come autumn, the seed heads burst into a textural and tactile frenzy, producing feathery pompoms, like cottonwool bolls, along the length of their growth.

'deer have always been important symbols at this time of the year'

Fig 44 The stag was an important motif in pagan and early medieval art. At its most basic, the deer was the servant/master/emblem of Herne the Hunter, the protective spirit of the woodland. In an age when life still depended on hunting to eat, the stag was both feared and revered, honoured and slaughtered. Any of these motifs, suggested by 8th/9th-century Anglo-Saxon embroidery motifs, could be worked similarly to that in Plate 61.

Floating embroidery is the key to their interpretation (see Stitch variations, page 135).

In Plate 62, the wild clematis (*Clematis vitalba*) is shown as the main feature of a small study (it is also featured in October, Plate 63, page 96). Floating embroidery works well to interpret a variety of effects and can be adapted to create different impressions. Depending on the thickness of the tool used to hold the thread away from the background fabric (see Fig 45), a more or less flamboyant, free effect is created – the broader the tool used, the more ebullient the meandering thread. Likewise, the choice of thread and colour can completely change the ambience of a study. A similar tracing to that used for this embroidery (Plate 62) is used in December (Plate 79, page 122) to create an entirely different effect.

As September ebbs and the nights lengthen we feel more inclined to detailed work. In this chapter we have looked at intricate, demanding techniques that alter the perspective of their subjects. Close-up, more detailed studies move into the realm of cellular analysis (Plates 59 and 60). Plate 61 takes Anglo-Saxon design into a more contemporized setting, and in Plate 62 we begin an exploration of floating embroidery that will be continued throughout the months to come. October will take us deeper into the realms of the autumnal supernatural . . .

'floating embroidery works well to interpret a variety of effects and can be adapted to create different impressions'

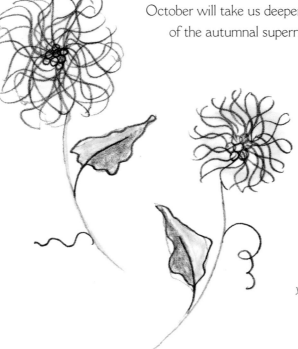

Fig 45 Floating embroidery is described in Stitch variations, page 135. What you choose to use to hold the thread away from the background fabric affects the outcome of the stitch. If you use a thick implement, such as your finger or a stubby felt-tipped pen, the loops of floating work will be more pronounced and longer (left). A thinner implement, such as a pencil or knitting needle will give a more subtle effect (right).

Plate 62 *Compare this study with Plate 79 (December, page 122): the same basic design is used but changes of colour and texture alter the final image. The fine floss silk used in the majority of studies in this book is usually laid flat and smooth on the surface of the back-ground fabric. (I don't use a laying tool but if you are more comfortable doing so, you are in good company – Japanese embroidery is always worked with one.) Here, however, the floss is allowed to 'fragment' on the floating embroidery to emphasize the ragged, flyaway nature of the subject.*
12.75 x 9cm (5 x 3½in)

OCTOBER

'Then came October full of merry glee' wrote Edmund Spenser in his epic poem 'The Faerie Queene', and there is, indeed, a piquancy to October that lifts the spirits before the onset of winter. Perhaps the unexpected brightness of the leaves – the Viking name for these days was the 'Yellow Month' – or maybe the onset of cosy fire-lit evenings (the Anglo-Saxons called it 'Winterfylleth'), the falling of winter gives humans and animals alike a glow of contentment. And then comes Hallowe'en! The Celtic new year arrived with the festival of Samhain; the fires that were to burn unquenched throughout the coming season were kindled, sacrifices made and the Eve of All Hallows, 31 October, became the Christian equivalent.

In the countryside, colours begin to fade with the ebbing of the month, textures becoming all important. The traveller's joy, which began its reign in September, now shares the hedgerow with old-man's beard (great willowherb) (Plate 63, left). Birds and animals take their tiny seeds as any food is at a premium now when the countdown to winter is underway. In field and woodland fungi raise their strange heads, appearing literally overnight – the ghosts of many a supernatural tale.

Don't be afraid to experiment with strange colours and textures: purple against black, maroon with old gold, otherworldly blue and turquoise with mulberry and mauve. Explore tactile, three-dimensional effects – the bursting seed heads of plants, gossamer plumes of feathers and the deep, pitted contours of toadstools (Plate 66). At this strange time of the year rules are there to be broken. The ill-fortuned opal is October's shadowy gemstone, thistle its challenging wildflower (Fig 46).

OF MICE AND . . .

'It's Punkie Night tonight, it's Punkie Night tonight,
Gie us a candle, gie us a light.'

(Traditional rhyme)

St Luke's Day, 18 October, has long been
associated with folklore, though latterly much eclipsed by
the more commercially viable Hallowe'en. 'St Luke's
Little Summer' refers to a spell of fine weather that often
occurs at around this date, and traditionally it was a good
time for maids to choose a husband. Divinations and
spells were cast to identify likely candidates and ensure
that they 'popped the question'. On St Crispin's Day,
25 October, the patron saint of shoemakers was
remembered (Crispin was a shoemaker in the
reign of the Roman Emperor Diocletian,
martyred for his Christian beliefs). A
traditional saying, 'the twenty-fifth of
October, the twenty-fifth of October,
cursed be the cobbler who goes to bed
sober!' ensured a good time was had by all.
Since 1415, St Crispin's Day has also been
remembered as the date of the Battle of
Agincourt, a famous victory for the English which was
celebrated annually for several centuries after the event.
With few flowers available to decorate for such
celebrations, country folk fell back on those plants that
festooned the hedgerows in abundance – dried hops,
traveller's joy and old-man's beard were obvious
favourites (Plate 63). What they lacked in colour was
made up for in texture, and we can use their inspiration

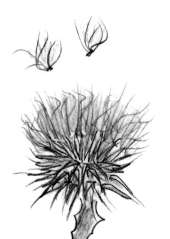

*Fig 46 Floating embroidery could be used
again to suggest the gossamer of thistledown
(left). Work the flower in bloom (right) in
straight stitching. The bulbous body of the
thistle itself is suggested by chevron stitching
(see Stitch variations, page 135 and Helen M.
Stevens' Embroidered Flowers, D&C, 2000).*

*Plate 63 (page 96) The tiny seeds of the old-man's beard (great
willowherb) are surrounded by fine filaments designed to catch the breeze
and bear the seed away – the same principle of dispersal as used by the
traveller's joy. They can be worked similarly but on a much smaller scale
(see Fig 48). The blue tit can be initially sketched to a geometric pattern
with triangles forming the principle shapes, softened by further detailing
(see Fig 47). Add details of large individual feathers into your sketch but
leave the finest of features to the embroidery – overlaid, softening feather
work need not be suggested at drawing board stage.*
Embroidery shown life-size 26.5 x 19cm (10¹/₂ x 7¹/₂in)

*'in the countryside,
colours begin to fade with the
ebbing of the month, textures
becoming all important'*

to create a marvellous evocation of late autumn.

A simple left-hand framework of stems and stalks, topped with the appropriate seed head and cases is sketched first. This could be used to frame any figure at the centre of the piece – in Plate 63 I have chosen a blue tit in flight hoping to snatch a flyaway seed (see also Fig 47). Give yourself an idea of the extent of the framing detail to be added to make sure that it sits comfortably within the overall design, and transfer the basic outline on to your fabric, with just a suggestion of the details to follow – these will be worked freehand. Work the framework and featured central element first, leaving the floating embroidery towards the end of the project as there is less chance of snagging the delicate fibres if the majority of the piece is already completed. See Fig 48 for a detailed description of the working of the old-man's beard. A few seeds in flight, eddying around the blue tit, add movement and interest to the piece. Keep them well spaced – the time has not yet arrived for a snowstorm!

In Plate 64 a framework element has again been used to great effect to 'cocoon' the central figure – in this case a dormouse (*Muscardinus avellanarius*) just beginning his long period of winter hibernation. In times gone by, the common dormouse – also called the hazel dormouse as it is extremely fond of hazelnuts – was a familiar animal in the countryside and often kept as a pet. 'What shall I call my dear little dormouse?

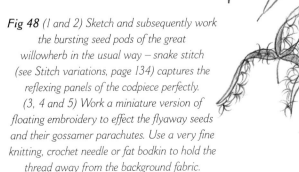

Fig 47 *It is important to look at a subject before you even begin to rough it out. The little blue tit in flight (Plate 63) is a series of triangles – beak, head, wings, tail – just get it down on paper (top). Now add a few details: where are the primary feathers? what colour is the crown/back/wing (middle)? Only when you are ready to transfer the design on to your fabric need you worry about real detail and then it is helpful to have as much as possible – head markings, individual feathers and so on (bottom). The more you can give yourself as a guide to stitching, the easier that most important aspect of the work will become.*

Fig 48 *(1 and 2) Sketch and subsequently work the bursting seed pods of the great willowherb in the usual way – snake stitch (see Stitch variations, page 134) captures the reflexing panels of the codpiece perfectly. (3, 4 and 5) Work a miniature version of floating embroidery to effect the flyaway seeds and their gossamer parachutes. Use a very fine knitting, crochet needle or fat bodkin to hold the thread away from the background fabric.*

Of mice and . . . - *October 99*

Plate 64 I have a beautiful hazel bush in my garden, part of an ancient hedge at least 200 years old and home to at least one dormouse who shares the nuts with passing squirrels (see November, Plate 69, page 106). Dormice can be encouraged into the garden by growing such shrubs and by increasing the number of tit-boxes in their generally vicinity as these have been known to house hibernating dormice though the long winter months. Here, a touch of metallic gold and silver suggests the frosts to come.
15.25 x 11.5cm (6 x 4¹/₂in)

'in times gone by, the common dormouse was a familiar animal in the countryside and often kept as a pet'

His eyes are small, but his tail is e-nor-mouse' asked Christopher Robin in A.A Milne's delightful story, *When We Were Very Young*.

Today, the little fellow is a good deal less common as, once again, his natural habitat has fallen victim to modern farming methods. The sweep of radial *opus plumarium* describing his tightly curled form is interrupted only by closed eyes (no highlight) and paws, whiskers are superimposed in long straight stitches – the same fine gauge of thread used on the old-man's beard but to very different effect.

Mice also feature strongly in some of A.A. Milne's lesser-known work. In his short poem 'Missing', Christopher Robin asks if anyone has seen '. . . a small sort of mouse, a dear little brown one, he came from the country, he wasn't a town one . . .' and is worried by what he 'could possibly find to eat, all lonely in a London street'. He need not have worried: mice whether town or country cousins rarely go hungry (Plate 65). The wood mouse (*Apodemus sylvaticus*), also called the long-tailed field mouse, is probably Britain's most widespread mammal. It thrives almost anywhere, from remote mountainsides to urban gardens – the latter often causing the uninitiated to think that house mice have moved in. They are, however, quite different: golden-brown to the house mouse's grey fur and completely odourless. Almost perfect (temporary) house guests, as many cat owners will know!

Nature is extraordinary. What we might think to be conflicting signals are somehow understood by wild creatures: the red that signals 'I'm ripe, eat me', can also mean 'I'm poisonous, leave me alone', but the two are rarely confused and the infamous fly agaric toadstool (*Amantia muscaria*), much-beloved seat of many a garden gnome, is shunned as foodstuff even with the coming of winter. The white spots on its crimson cap are remnants of a membrane that covers the immature fungus as it emerges from the earth. As the 'umbrella' opens, the membrane fragments and is left speckling the cap, standing slightly proud. No Dalmatian dog technique here then as we want the spots to look quite separate from their background.

Plate 65 A few last ears of grain are often still to found in protected areas into October, a useful addition to pre-winter preparations. As in the two previous Plates, the naturally growing framework of the subject surrounds the central character. Again, this format could be sketched geometrically to find a correct ratio of size between the two.
10.75 x 10cm (4¹/₄ x 4in)

Plate 66 Into the woods . . .
10 x 12cm (4 x 4³/₄in)

If working on a pale background, shadow line the toadstool in the usual way, also shadowing under the individual spots, then work these first, keeping straight stitches on a horizontal alignment. Flood the red *opus plumarium* around the spots, working towards a diffuse growing point at the top of the cap and voiding around each spot. The resulting effect is one of the white markings resting on top of their base.

As many country dwellers will know, there are far more fungi that are edible (and delicious too) than are poisonous, but few of us are foolhardy enough to take a chance unless we are real experts. There is also something otherworldly about fungi; their way of appearing overnight often in secluded spots and their association with the little people (fairy rings are the result of the underground spreading of spores) have left us with uneasy folk memories which are hard to shake off. Plate 66 shows a collection of colourful examples.

'in field and woodland fungi raise their strange heads, appearing literally overnight – the ghosts of many a supernatural tale'

The yellow *Cantharellus cibarius* (centre) is well known as the chanterelle, much sought after in cooking (and easily dried for storage), but it could well be confused with the Roll Rim, a similar yellow fungus that is highly poisonous – its Latin name *involutus* giving a clue to the violent spasms caused by eating it. Neither of the other two large toadstools shown are regarded as poisonous either; *Suillus luteus* (left) is commonly eaten, though the peppery flesh of the *Russula atropurpurea* (right) is unappealing. One of the greatest joys of fungi can be their names – the little fairy toadstools in the foreground are Trooping Crumble Caps (*Coprinus disseminatus*).

Generally speaking, work radial *opus plumarium* towards the centre of the cap of the fungi to create a realistic effect, taking your cue by establishing exactly where that centre point is (Fig 49). On the central and right-hand subjects in Plate 66, this core is hidden inside the concave, funnel shape of the caps. Work your stitches flowing into it, applying the opposite angle principle (see page 134). Seed stitching and straight stitching will suggest the gills and stems. Working on black, voiding provides the necessary shadow lines, but deep grey areas of shade beneath the overhang of the caps are also effective. On a pale background the use of a shadow line is all important, as shown in Plate 66.

To suggest the disappearance of the spider's web into the mouth of the right-hand funnel, I have calculated the angles required for the web to meet the inner wall at the appropriate point and allowed the stitches to terminate abruptly at the foremost void.

With the coming of Hallowe'en, spooky subjects are irresistible. Plate 66 has already taken us into the wild woods, so what other subjects can we find in nature to capture the spirit of 'Punkie Night'? Punkies, bogeys and pookas were all thought to be elemental spirits of the night, glimpsed out of the corner of an eye or perhaps seen more fully after a long sojourn at the local inn. Certainly the death's-head hawkmoth (*Acherontia atropos*) might well have been confused with a ghostly apparition; with a wingspan (and caterpillar) of up 12.5cm (5in) they arrive in the autumn, at one time to the consternation of potato pickers, as the hawkmoth's favourite foods are members of the *Solanum* family. The scientific name of the moth is given for the Greek goddess Atropos who ruled over matters of mortal life and death. The unmistakable 'death's-head' pattern on the adult's body explains the association. Potatoes, like other solanum are 'nightshades', and the death's-head hawkmoth is attracted to all of them, including the deadly nightshade *Atropa belladonna*, also named for the goddess of mortality. Against a black background 'hung all over with purple and pall' ('Down in Yon Forest', a traditional Corpus Christie carol) – could there be a more atmospheric study? (Plate 67).

Fig 49 Fungi are fascinating. The growing point for your opus plumarium *is the apex of the umbrella – this may be on the top (as in the two upper drawings) or in the centre of a concave depression (as in the lower drawings). In every case, make sure that your stitches flow smoothly towards it, applying the opposite angle principle as necessary.*

'*punkies, bogeys and
pookas were all thought to be
elemental spirits of the night*'

Though larger and with a somewhat more complicated body pattern, the death's-head hawkmoths are worked essentially similarly to the elephant hawkmoth in Plate 53 (August, page 82). The 'death's-head' pattern on the back is worked in multiple Dalmatian dog technique – the black-on-black features of the 'skull' first, then the skull itself, flooded around the black, and finally surrounded by the gunmetal grey of the body. Lower segments are worked separately, leaving a void between each, which is then infilled with a surface-couched black and gold plied thread, used again for the antennae. The pale, deep and even deeper purples of the belladonna bud, flower and berry merge tantalizingly with the black background fabric, only emerging fully when caught by light at just the right angle.

Amulets, tokens and charms were all needed to ward off the perils of Punkie Night, and from time immemorial the spiritual powers of certain creatures were sought and thought to be harnessed within such charms to give the wearer the attributes of his tribe's chosen 'totem'. Eagles were known to be strong and far sighted (essential protection against the supernatural), fearless and noble. They were popular subjects in Viking and Anglo-Saxon art. Plate 68 is adapted from patterns found on the Sutton Hoo ship burial treasure from the 7th century. The basic outline (Fig 50) is laid down simply in red stem stitch, then embellished with split stitching and the addition of semiprecious stones and beads together with meandering surface couching. Thick gold cord is also surface couched as borders to the various concentric circles.

Hallowe'en, 31 October, the eve of 'All Hallows', itself the day before 'All Souls', is the gate into winter, but before it quite closes behind us November promises some last surprises.

*Plate 68 Sodalite (dark blue) and peridot (pale green) are two semiprecious stones that traditionally calm and clear the mind, relieving stress, stimulating and strengthening both body and soul – an ideal antidote to fears of the supernatural at Hallowe'en! The eagle's eyes are represented by faux pearls, each stylized bird outlined in tiny seed beads. A piece such as this could be mounted on a piece of stiff cardboard (cut exactly to size) and a brooch fitting stitched to the reverse.
7cm (2³/₄in) diameter*

Fig 50 Among the treasures found at the Sutton Hoo ship burial – the tumulus of an Anglo-Viking king – was a great shield boss bearing an emblem of eagles interspersed with enamel and precious metals and stones. I have interpreted this in Plate 68. This basic pattern could be embroidered in many ways – let the spirit of Hallowe'en move you!

Plate 67 (opposite) Work the long bars on the moths' wings as elongated Dalmatian dog spots and flood the main field of colour in around them as this is easier than working fragmented strata. Simple directional opus plumarium *describes the deadly nightshade leaves, while a highlight created by a few straight, overlaid ticking stitches suggests the shiny surface of the berries.*
21.5 x 11.5cm (8¹/₂ x 4¹/₂in)

NOVEMBER

'Blot-monath', the Blood Month, was the Anglo-Saxon name for November and, perhaps strangely, blood and tears seem to be the legacy of its thirty-day span. All Souls' Day, when the living remember the departed, falls on 2 November; the anniversary of the Gunpowder Plot and the gory demise of Guy Fawkes in 1605, is re-enacted in Britain on the 5 November; and Armistice Day, recalling those fallen in too many bloody wars arrives internationally with 11 November. The one bright light amid the gloom is the United States' Thanksgiving Day, celebrated on the last Thursday of the month.

In past centuries, when death was regarded as but part of life, November's more morbid associations were treated with a levity that we might find hard to understand. Bonfires built at the beginning of the month were thought to release the dead from purgatory for the duration of their burning, and 'soul-cakes' were baked to celebrate the event. Heinous crimes committed on 'Mischief Night' were traditionally unpunishable and on 'nutcrack night', another somewhat moveable feast at around the beginning of the month in Suffolk, England, hazelnuts (Plate 69, left) and apple pips were put on the fire to represent a girl and her sweetheart: if they exploded, good sexual fireworks would ensue in the relationship; if they burned dully the boy would be cuckolded within the year and death might follow.

Look for colours and textures that will light the way to the festive season: red and gold, chestnut and silver, the auburn-yellow of topaz (November's gemstone) and the many petalled and faceted chrysanthemum (its traditional flower, see Plate 71 and Fig 53). Celebrate the strangeness of this otherworldly month.

LEST WE FORGET

'Remember, remember, the fifth of November:
Gunpowder, treason and plot . . .' (Traditional rhyme)

At the eleventh hour of the eleventh day of the
eleventh month, 1918, the guns finally fell silent on what had
been the world's bloodiest conflict: the Great War was over.
Those surviving in the barren, muddy trenches must have
found it hard to believe that in England there was still, in the
words of Rupert Brooke's poem 'The Old Vicarage,
Granchester', 'peace and holy quiet' to which they might
return; that the inviolable cycle of the seasons had rolled
forward to yet another November, that fruit and nuts still
hung on late-clad trees, and small animals went about their
everyday business of preparation for winter (Plate 69).

For all its darkness, increasingly long cold evenings and
late foggy mornings, there is a beauty to be found in the
November countryside. Now, at last, we begin to see
the elegant, skeletal outlines of trees long hidden by
foliage as frost strips that last vestige of summer.
And yet there are reminders of the spring to come:
the hazel bush (*Corylus avellana*) whilst
bearing its luscious sugar-
brown nuts already supports
the immature male catkins
that will burst into new life
in February. Like the
dormouse (by now well into
his hibernation, see October,
Plate 64, page 100) the grey
squirrel is grateful for its largesse.

Plate 69 illustrates three different approaches to 'finding
the core' of a subject. On the squirrel, the radial *opus
plumarium* sweeps to his nose; on the hazelnuts and the

'look for colours
and textures that will light the
way to the festive season: red and
gold, chestnut and silver, the
auburn-yellow of topaz'

*Fig 51 The 'pip-tip' of a fruit or nut is all
important for the embroiderer. Here, X marks
the spot. Make sure that your stitches flow
radially towards this point, whether it is at the
centre of the motif or at the edge – full-faced or
profile, the growing point is still the core of the
motif. Top: hazelnuts in their frilly 'collars';
below, snowberries.*

***Plate 69** (page 106) Beginning in early autumn, the grey squirrel
(*Sciurus carolinensis*) moults the yellow-brown elements of his grizzled
fur, replacing them with pale silvery-grey, giving him a much more uniform
appearance. By November, only nose, paws and the odd streak in his tail
breaks up the silver and white.
Embroidery shown life-size 24 x 20.25cm (9¹/₂ x 8in)*

snowberry (*Symphoricarpos rivularis*) fruit it needs to radiates towards the 'pip-tip' of the subject (Fig 51). This knotty little point is where the flower originally fell away from the pollinated fruiting body and it decides the overall shape of the subsequent berry or nut. By working your stitches towards this point rather than the stalk, a more accurate interpretation of this type of subject is achieved. Compare it with the working of the sloes in Plate 57 (see page 86); these are rounded, the 'pip-tip' indistinguishable in embroidery just as it is on the sloe itself.

The common hazel has been one of humankind's most perpetually useful shrubs for millennia. A framework of hazel covered by animal hides formed the fishing coracles of the prehistoric Welsh 3,000 years ago and throughout the centuries, as the countryman's needs changed, so the hazel was there to offer assistance. 'Wattles' cut from the coppiced tree created panels which were then 'daubed' with mud to build houses, while 'springels', again from the coppice, attached the thatch to its roof. Hazel was used to pen sheep, woven into laid hedgerows, stripped for use as bean poles and pea sticks, and cut as beaters' switches for shooting. Traditionally, country wives used long hazel props to raise their laundry lines and hazel faggots to fuel their bread ovens. A well-established hazel bush in a hedge suggests considerable age. In November, the few remaining leaves have turned a rich orange-yellow flecked with green, and are tinted with a delicate pink, one of the autumn woodland's most unique shades. On a large leaf, work the basic colours in bold areas of directional *opus plumarium* and then overlay towards the edges with shooting stitches (see page 135) in some of the more unusual hues.

Country lads returning home after World War I found a changed environment. The fabric of society had unravelled in the four years of conflict and many country ways were gone forever. When the first anniversary of Armistice Day came in 1919, a new annual traditional began: two minutes of silence were observed at 11am to remember everyone and everything that had been lost. The practice continues to this day, the poppies of Flanders becoming forever associated with the fallen. Plate 70 is a simple study capturing that spirit of remembrance. The poppies, out of their usual summer context, are framed with reflexed grasses (see Fig 52). Dark and light green contrast sharply to bring their subdued, muted shapes into focus. Such a design could be used as a loving tribute in a piece of church, or any other commemorative, embroidery.

Plate 70 The common poppy is the variety that grew most commonly in the fields of Flanders and has become stylized as the symbol of remembrance. Its two smaller and two larger petals are arranged uniquely among flowers (see Fig 52). Their tissue-paper texture should be worked in a finer silk than usual – allowing a little of the background fabric to show through the embroidery adds to the translucent effect. 10.25 x 10.25cm (4 x 4in)

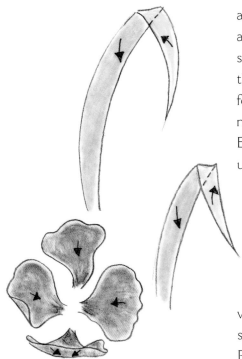

Fig 52 Long-bladed leaves (Plate 70) require the careful use of snake stitch. Always work with the curve (arrows indicate the direction of stitching) and imagine a continuation of the lower outline behind the flexing blade (shown by the dashed line) to ensure that a smooth 'flip-over' is effected. The common poppy consists of four petals: two larger outer lobes cupping two smaller inner ones. Imagine them taken apart to make sure that you effect the correct angle of radial opus plumarium.

Church embroidery, reflecting, of course, the ecclesiastical seasons, is a study in its own right. Apart from seasonal hangings – for the altar, lecterns and so on – and vestments for the officiating clergy, most churches both large and small have their own personal collection of textiles; from lovingly tent-stitched kneelers, to Mother's Union banners, and the 'napery' associated with the Eucharist. Some churches have special connections with particular festivals, saints' days and other major events in their own history, with needlework to match. These more individual pieces are a joy to discover. At Ely Cathedral in Cambridgeshire, England, a pair of gilt chairs was specially upholstered and embroidered for a visit of Queen Elizabeth II and Prince Philip. Worked in the Jacobean style, they inspired my design in Plate 71 – a stylized celebration of Guy Fawkes' Night.

Guy Fawkes' Night, Bonfire Night, Firework Night, The Fifth of November – call the celebration what you will – is a particularly British institution. In 1605, a group of disaffected Catholics led by Robert Catesby and assisted by Guido Fawkes attempted to blow up King James I, together with the whole of his Parliament. The plan became known when one of their sympathizers warned a relative who had been due to attend the opening of Parliament on the fateful day. The cellars of the Houses of Parliament were searched and Fawkes caught red-handed with the barrels of gunpowder. His co-conspirators were apprehended, several tortured and executed. It is an irony that Guy himself is the only name chiefly remembered in association with the plot, though he was really little more than a factotum. It is his grisly execution that is re-enacted with the burning of his effigy every November – though the tradition of 'passing through fire' slots neatly into much earlier rituals of the coming of winter, celebrated from pagan times.

Taking my cue from the design of a similar piece of early 17th-century English embroidery (at the time of the Gunpowder Plot patterns were deliciously flamboyant), I abandoned traditional colours for bright, flaming-red foliage – the bonfire – and gold, coiling florals – fireworks! Worked in pure silk and real gold thread, this piece has a wonderful lustre and richness effected by simple *opus plumarium* and surface couching.

The stylized flowers of Jacobean design – often executed in stumpwork – are not always easy to identify. The three chosen for Plate 71 (left to right) suggest clematis, chrysanthemum and columbine, all of which would have been known to the embroiderers of the day. The essential elements of each flower have been extrapolated

Fig 53 Chinese design often uses the stylized chrysanthemum – symbolic of joviality and ease – variously interpreted, as here.

and reinterpreted, perhaps in ways that would have originally shown off complicated techniques to their best advantage. The tradition of stylizing floral and foliate subjects is by no means unique to the Jacobeans (see Fig 53). Working on a black background gives a modern twist to the piece and emphasizes the idea of night-time, fire and festival.

In 1606, just one year after James I survived the infamous Gunpowder Plot, a group of speculators acquired a Royal Charter to establish the Virginia Company with rights to trade with the colonies of the New World. North America was open for business! Settlers, however, had hard times ahead; none more so than the Plymouth colony who set sail from that port in September 1620 aboard the *Mayflower*. After ten weeks of gruelling sailing, they landed at Cape Cod (by chance just outside the jurisdiction of the Virginia Colony). A pact was drawn up to combine 'together into a civil body

Plate 71 Scrolling foliate and floral designs were popular in Elizabethan England and continued in favour through early Stuart and Jacobean decades, though the emphasis on the stem-like curlicues may derive from medieval origins. Jackets, stomachers, sleeves, yokes and coifs were often covered in a repeat pattern, and its use was extended to furnishings too, as bed hangings, curtains and upholstery all disappeared beneath a riot of plant life.
18.5 x 17cm (7¼ x 6¾in)

Plate 72 The blue jay is also a resident of Canada, where Thanksgiving is celebrated in October. Like many corvids, it is garrulous and attracted to bright objects and will share human habitation only when there is a benefit to be had – stealing food set out for smaller birds is a favourite trick. Blending more than one shade in the needle (as with the squirrel, Plate 69) is useful here, too. On the breast of the bird, pinkish-buff graduates slowly into white as mixing progresses.
12.25 x 12.25cm (5 x 5in)

Fig 54 The 'pip-tip' of an acorn is its apex and stitches should flow upward towards it (X marks the spot). The little 'pipe' in which the nut nestles can be worked in massed seed stitches. Where a bolder but more distant outline is required, straighter stitches may be used (Plates 72 and 73).

politic' and to frame 'just and equal laws' and in December the New England town of Plymouth was founded. A hard struggle with nature ensued but in the autumn of 1621 they celebrated a 'Thanksgiving' for their first harvest – an annual tradition that survives to this day on the last Thursday of November.

Thanksgiving is as unique to the USA as Bonfire Night is to the British and its traditional accoutrements, such as pumpkin pie, are now just as well known. To those early settlers, however, their new home must have appeared strange and unfamiliar. New species of animals, birds and trees, startling in their diversity and colour were to be encountered – some with echoes of distant homelands. The blue jay (*Cyanocitta cristata*) (Plate 72) is the New World counterpart of Europe's common jay (*Garrulus glandarius*) (Plate 73) – a slightly smaller, slimmer version of this colourful, cocky little member of the crow family. Now a familiar resident of suburbs, parks and gardens in most eastern North American cities, it was originally a bird of woodland and forest and must have been a common sight as early settlers cleared the ground for their first homesteads. Both birds are a joy for embroiderers.

In Plate 72 the blue jay is shown on the North American blackjack oak (*Quercus marilandica*). Its small acorns (Fig 54) would have immediately singled it out as a member of the familiar oak family but the unlobed leaves would have been a surprise to early naturalists as they documented the species of the new continent. The autumnal shades of the leaves complement the vivid blue of the bird beautifully and this simple study needs no further embellishment. Similarly, the common jay in Plate 73 on his perch of European oak (*Quercus robur*) makes a pleasing and appropriate pair to the former piece. 'Feather work' – *opus plumarium* – is, of course, the perfect medium for the birds, variously incorporating into the basic technique areas of Dalmatian dog spotting, ticking and straight stitching.

With the end of November comes two saints' days. St Catherine, patron saint of lace-makers and spinsters (in the sense of their profession not their marital status) is remembered on 25 November. Colourful threads and ribbons were once hung from a representation of the wheel on which she was martyred. Scotland's patron saint, Andrew, brings the month to an end on 30 November. About now the age-old question 'will it be a white Christmas?' begins to be aired. According to country folklorists: 'Ice in November to bear a duck, nothing much after but slush and muck'. So now you know!

'the autumnal shades of the leaves complement the vivid blue of the bird beautifully'

Plate 73 Once you have spotted a common jay it is probable that you will be able to find it again as they are territorial and favour given areas. Even their flight patterns are regularly repeated. In one stand of woodland near my home I know exactly where the resident jay will emerge and disappear as he goes about his day-to-day routine. If you watch patiently you may be able to establish favourite perches, too. Then, a quick photo or sketch will allow you to refer back to your own reference matter when you are at design stage. His cocky, wide-legged 'jizz' is unmistakeable.
12.25 x 11.5cm (5 x 4¹/₂in)

Plate 74 *Many oaks hold on to their leaves well into the winter in calm conditions, but high winds will strip the most tenacious branch during a really stormy autumn. Even so, a few twigs retain the odd brown and gold remnant of summer all the way to Christmas and beyond. There is a surprising amount of colour left in the winter countryside – red, russet and orange speckle the hedgerow, all possible titbits for the robin. Early winter crops begin to show green as early as November. Touches of white suggest melting snow.*
Embroidery shown life-size 25.5 x 40.75 (10 x 16in)

DECEMBER

December was the last month of the Romans' ten-month year and it still marks the end of the year for us too. Christian Anglo-Saxons called it 'heligh-monath', the Holy-month in which Christmas fell, but this celebration was also an incarnation of the great pagan midwinter festival: the Solstice. Woden, the Norse god, flew across the sky at this time, his chariot drawn by fabulous beasts, to distribute gifts to his faithful followers. In a chariot drawn by cats, the goddess Freyja followed suit, just as Santa Claus and his reindeer have for more recent generations. The Roman feast of Saturnalia began the tradition of bringing greenery into the home to celebrate the season.

Whatever the origins of our own festivals, this season can be nothing if not celebratory. Perhaps it is within the heart of all us to want to mark the turning of the year. In Australia the festive season coincides with the summer solstice, so what better reason to celebrate? It is a time for fun and games, for silliness and, sometimes, stillness: a moment to contemplate the year gone and the year to come.

There is no need to hesitate in the choice of fabulous, forthright colours. Red is the colour of the season, with startling white, shimmering silver, glorious greens and glamorous golds. Textures can be as sumptuous as they are surprising – a Christmas fairy as ethereal as gossamer, as bright as zircon (December's gem, Plate 75, left), her hiding place as vibrant as the holly, ivy or poinsettia – traditionally this month's flower (Plate 81), though it is not a flower at all. In the words of Charles Dickens' Tiny Tim in 'A Christmas Carol', 'God bless us – every one!'

THE HOLLY AND THE IVY

*'A jug of Christmas ale, Sir, will make our voices ring,
And money in our pockets makes a very pretty ring.'*

(Traditional song)

Christmas festivities traditionally begin in Europe with St Nicholas' Day, 6 December. Nicholas was the patron saint of children, noted for the giving of gifts, and his feast-day fell conveniently near to the time when Woden, the Norse god, hurtled across the night sky bestowing his favours. When Christian rulers outlawed his veneration, St Nick, Santa Claus, stepped smoothly into his shoes – and sleigh!

'silver metallics and translucent cellophane threads suggest frost and ice'

At Saturnalia, the Roman master and servant changed places for the duration of the festival; this might be the origin of the Christian tradition, quite widespread in the Middle Ages, of electing a 'Boy Bishop' for the Christmas period. Appointed on St Nicholas' Day, he was enthroned in Episcopal splendour and executed all the offices of Bishop (with exception of celebrating the Mass) until 28 December, Holy Innocents' Day, a date that commemorates the slaughter of Bethlehem's children by Herod. Also during the medieval period, great trees were erected in city streets to be danced around and decorated – so Prince Albert, generally credited with introducing Christmas trees to England in 1847 was, in fact, resurrecting a much earlier practice. It is interesting that the Christmas Fairy still often replaces the more Christianized holy star of Bethlehem.

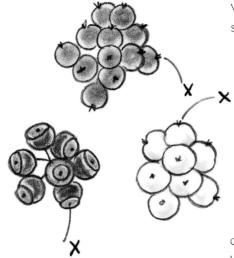

Fig 55 *More berries, all redolent of the season and each with easily recognisable 'pip-tips' (X marks the spot). Holly berries (top) are round, bullet-like, self-coloured little motifs worked towards a substantial core, while the mistletoe (right) is a fleshier berry, white, delicately flushed with green, again flowing to a central growing point. The ivy berries (left) are a slightly different proposition. Little round 'caps' with a central 'pip-tip' surmount each deep purple globe – work this cap first and flow the rest of the motif towards it. On black, void between cap and berry; on pale fabric both should be carefully shadow lined (see Plate 75).*

Plate 75 *(page 116) Holly (*Ilex aquifolium*), ivy (*Hedera helix*) and mistletoe (*Viscum album*) each have a claim to supernatural influence as the festive season approaches. It was considered highly unlucky to cut down a holly tree, ivy was thought to be magical as two types of leaves grew on the same plant (lobed and unlobed), whilst the strange ability of mistletoe to live on its host tree without imparting any harm merited its respect – and many magical applications. Kissing under the mistletoe is still the best-known Druid custom.*
Embroidery shown life-size 26.5 x 18.5cm (10¹/₂ x 7¹/₄in)

Holly, ivy and mistletoe (Plate 75), together with the yule-log (brought into the house on Christmas Eve and, once lit, not allowed to go out until completely consumed), are all remnants of earlier rituals. Holly and ivy are now widely accepted and brought into churches to decorate them for Christmas services, though holly was once thought to be the witches' tree. Mistletoe is still often regarded as inappropriate in a church setting as its Druidic associations are too widely remembered. In Plate 75 these three plants are woven together by the magic of the Christmas Fairy to create the very fabric of the festive season.

Work out your palette of colours carefully before beginning a foliate design such as this. Much of the charm of the piece lies in its simplicity and too abrupt a change in shading or too great a diversity in the 'families' of colours chosen can spoil the effect. Similarly, stitch lengths are fairly uniform – the dimensions of individual leaves are not dissimilar, so try to graduate your stitches smoothly. Berries in each case are worked towards the 'pip-tip' (Fig 55 and Fig 54, page 112): small, compact, bullet shapes, stitches closely abutted to prevent the background fabric showing through. Work the surface couching, taking care that the couching stitches themselves are roughly equidistant (though they will need to converge slightly where tendrils coil tightly).

In the foliate sections of this study, therefore, there is nothing too complicated to challenge the embroiderer – coiling stems are worked in stem stitch or surface couching (as discussed), leaves in directional *opus plumarium* and berries in radial work. The prickles of the holly leaves are effected by working long straight stitches in a fine thread extending beyond the apex of each sharp-toothed lobe (Fig 56) – keep the angle of the straight stitch exactly matching the directional work and, where appropriate, overlay across underlying stitches. Silver metallics and translucent cellophane threads suggest frost and ice, as also seen in Plate 76.

Fig 56 Holly leaves present a marvellous outline. Work directional opus plumarium *towards the elongated core, using opposite angle stitching where appropriate. Create the long prickles with a single fine straight stitch for each, worked at the same angle as the underlying embroidery.*

Plate 76 *A pine branch, festooned with silver tinsel in the shape of frosty cobwebs and supporting gold fir cones, heralds the coming of nature's own festive season. The pretty crested tit (*Parus cristatus*) relies on spiders' webs for its nesting material and stakes its claim for a desirable nest site early in the year.*
17.25 x 7.7cm (7 x 3in)

The fairy, however, presents more of a conundrum (Plate 77, detail of Plate 75 and also Fig 57). Like her sister the summer fairy (June, Plate 38, page 59), she is ethereal and the finest of speckling stitches create her body and hair, but worked on black these need to be worked very closely to block out the dulling effect of the dark background. Before working the stitches themselves, rub a white chalk pencil over the field to be covered as this will partially 'lift' the darkness and break up the density of the black ground material. Do not attempt too great a degree of detail on face, hands and feet as this little lady is from a place where the imagination reigns supreme – impressionism is the key to success here. Her wings are worked in honeycomb stitch overlaid with a cellophane thread. Her fairy dust is a potent mixture of seed beads, seed stitches and minute sequins.

Like the 'psychic' photographs of the 1920s and 1930s, a misty, swirling effect completes the image. This is achieved by overlaying a very finely teased gossamer of unspun raw silk over the fairy's lower body, trailing away behind her. This device is used again on the Christmas roses (*Helleborus niger*) in Plate 78.

Plate 77 (detail of Plate 75) Working the speckling stitches very closely can almost completely obscure the background fabric – leave a minute void between features. Detail shown: 7.5 x 5.5cm (3 x 2⅛in)

In common with many hellebores the Christmas rose is a winter bloomer; once established in the garden it will survive well from year to year, increasing as its self-seedlings come to maturity (it takes about three years for a new plant to flower). Hellebores have a romantic history often linked with the supernatural. The Romans chanted prayers to Apollo when lifting the plant – and kept an eye open for eagles for it was believed that if one was spotted at this inopportune time death would follow within the year. Large clumps of the Christmas rose beside an old cottage door are a link with past times when it would have been set by the threshold to ward off evil spirits.

Simple white radial *opus plumarium* describes the petals, whilst the pollen mass is an intermingling of yellow, orange and brick-red seed stitches surrounded by a corolla (in the shape of a narrow first strata) in bright green. Directional *opus plumarium* and straight stitches for leaves and grasses frame the blooms – over this lower element a fine swathe of unspun silk suggests the spectral mist of early winter morning, cellophane thread mingling with the silk.

Fig 57 This Christmas fairy is swathed in gossamer. In Plate 75 (and detail, Plate 77) this teased, unspun silk coils around her, disappearing where it cocoons her body behind her legs. Lay the silk over the motif and carefully cut it sheer at the perceived point of disappearance. The same could be effected behind her arm as suggested here (cuts are indicated by arrows).

As discussed earlier (May, page 51), the easiest way to acquire fine cellophane thread is to strip out the sparkling element from a blending filament (see Suppliers, page 136) and use it singly. Blending filaments come in a large variety of shades and colours, some with cellophane, some with metallic threads: the choice of what you use and where is as wide as your imagination allows – and in Plate 79 it has been allowed full rein. Compare this study with Plate 62 (September, page 95): the same basic sketch has been used, reversed, and interpreted in a wholly different colourway and choice of materials. Oh, yes, and the late-flying mayflies have turned into fairies! The floating embroidery of the traveller's joy (it can still be found in the hedgerow in December, often sparkling with frost) is worked in white and silver silk, together with pale icy-green cellophane strands, which has been used again for the gowns of the little sprites. Gold, white and red create a vivid burst of foliate colour, silver replacing the gold metallic thread couched as tendrils, centre and bottom.

Silver is the colour usually associated with the moon, starlight and the night sky generally. As midwinter approaches with the solstice on 21 December, the Northern Lights (Wulfendatter's Embroidery, see *Helen M. Stevens' World of Embroidery*, D&C, 2002) dance in the Scandinavian heavens. Freyja's chariot drawn by two cats, supposedly one tabby and white, one ginger and white,

'silver is the colour usually associated with the moon, starlight and the night sky generally'

Plate 79 A Christmas fantasy.
12.75 x 9cm (5 x 3¹/₂in)

circles the world and it is said that to enter the fairy world, you need only take a cat upon your knee, have a nipperkin of wine at your elbow, anoint both yourself and the cat with the sign of the cross in wine and recite 'Elves of the night, enchant my sight, your forms for to see in the pale moonlight'. This tradition inspired the last of my Anglo-Saxon quartet (Plate 80).

Like the other studies in this series (Plate 23 page 35, Plate 41 page 65 and Plate 68 page 105), this piece is worked in the style of the mid-Saxon period, in split-stitched silk and surface-couched silver and gold thread, the colour 'jigsaw' radiating from the sickle moon and consolidating into a stylized landscape. The popular visual riddle, often used by Anglo-Saxon artists, of the zoomorph's (in this case a cat) tongue turning into its own tail is also a feature (see Fig 58).

The feast day of St Thomas is also 21 December. Going 'a-Thomasing' on this date was, until the middle of the 19th century, a common practice allowing the poor to ask for alms without losing their dignity. It was gradually replaced by the tradition of Boxing Day when a Christmas 'box' or tip was given to tradesmen to thank them for their services

'over the festive season I always enjoy having a simple piece of work to turn to in quiet moments'

Fig 58 *A zoomorph is a curious beast that 'morphs' into and out of logical form and the expression was coined long before the advent of digital special effects. Here two zoomorphic motifs are apparently arranged symmetrically – but all is not as it seems: though the right-hand beast's tongue does, indeed, turn into its tail, the left-hand creature is a much more complicated affair. Trace this maze and you are in the company of puzzlers from the 8th century.*

Plate 80 *It is said that at the first Christmas a tabby cat played with a ball of wool to entertain the Baby Jesus in his manger crib and stopped him crying. To show her gratitude the Virgin laid the wool on the cat's forehead in the shape of an 'M' for Mary, and all true tabbies carry the mark to this day – certainly mine does! (See* The Myth and Magic of Embroidery, *D&C, 1999)*
6.25 x 5cm (2¹/₂ x 2in)

throughout the past year. In the same way, carol singing has largely replaced wassailing, but the object was the same – to collect money. A few days later country folk firmly believed that bees sung in their hives on Christmas Eve and the oxen knelt in their stalls, heads to the East.

Few of us have the time (or inclination) to wield a needle on Christmas Day, although over the festive season I always enjoy having a simple piece of work to turn to in quiet moments. What better than a study of poinsettia, December's flower (Plate 81)? Embroidering all the diverse studies for this book has been a joy but this striking portrait is almost my favourite. With a very limited palette of colours and just three stitch techniques (see caption) it encapsulates the essence of Christmas.

'with a limited palette of colours and just three stitch techniques it encapsulates the essence of Christmas'

The poinsettia (*Euphorbia pulcherrima*) is a Mexican species and in tropical gardens can grow to 3m (10ft) tall, but the plant widely grown for the Christmas trade in Europe and North America is the small variety 'Paul Mikkelsen'. Its showy 'flowers' are not flowers at all but large, petal-like bracts surrounding tiny insignificant blooms (rather like the clematis, see July, Plate 46, page 71). Bright scarlet, as shown here, or occasionally white (Fig 59), they remain in character for weeks – right over the

Christmas period and well into the New Year. That the flame-like bracts have become so popular at Christmas and New Year might not simply be due to their beauty: 'Burning the Bush' on New Year's Day was a ceremony once widely held where an old dry hawthorn was burnt to ward off evil spirits in the coming year. Sometimes, too, the mistletoe was taken down and burnt as the clock struck midnight.

'while nature unfurls with the circling seasons, we stitchers are never at a loss for inspiration'

As the wassail cup was passed around to toast the climax of the passing year, the Roman god Janus again looked forward to the months to come. We still celebrate the arrival of 1 January with New Year resolutions, determined to make it even better than the last.

While nature unfurls with the circling seasons, we stitchers are never at a loss for inspiration, and as our own celebrations and traditions continue to change and evolve we are privileged to record them in the most timeless and time-honoured medium of all – embroidery.

Fig 59 The white poinsettia is a pure, simple emblem of the season. This design could be worked on black, cream, green or red to capture the spirit of Christmas.

Plate 81 (right) Radial and directional opus plumarium *and stem stitch are the only techniques used in this lovely red poinsettia study. Two shades of red and green, light and dark respectively, on the upper and lower sides of the bracts and leaves effect an enormous diversity of shades as the light catches the stitching. Sometimes (and perhaps especially at Christmas) a return to simplicity really can be the best plan.*
19 x 14cm (7½ x 5½in)

MATERIALS

FABRIC

The choice of fabric and threads can greatly affect the ultimate appearance of any embroidery and, as with the choice of colourways, this should be at the discretion of the individual embroiderer. However, to achieve satisfactory results, some practical considerations do need to be borne in mind.

For so-called flat-work embroidery which must be worked in a frame, it is essential that the fabric chosen for the background does not stretch. If the fabric stretches even slightly while the embroidery is in progress, when taken out of the frame it will contract to its normal size and the embroidery will be distorted. It is also a good idea to look for a smooth, evenweave fabric. Suitable fabrics include:

- Cotton
- Polyester cotton ('Percale')
- Linen

Pure silk may also be used, but avoid types with too much 'slub' in the weave as this will interrupt the flow of the embroidery stitches.

The embroideries in this book have been worked on an inexpensive cotton/polyester fabric (sometimes called 'Percale') which is very lightweight. Poly-cotton mixes (evenweave) in a heavier weight are also ideal for use in this type of embroidery. Generally, larger pictures should be worked on heavier fabrics,

and small studies on lightweights, but this rule can, of course, be adapted to the particular needs of the project in question.

When choosing fabric, try to avoid any fabrics which have too loose a weave, as this will result in too many stitches vying for space in too few threads of warp and weft. As a general rule, if the weave is open enough to be used for counted thread embroidery, it will be too wide for us.

THREADS

A variety of threads are necessary to achieve diverse effects but the ultimate choice of which type to use on any specific area is a personal one. Any thread suitable for flat-work embroidery may be used for any of the techniques in this book. Natural fibres are easier to use than synthetics and these include cotton, floss silk and twisted silk.

Pure silks and cottons are available in a glorious variety of colours and textures. Clockwise from bottom left: stranded cottons, stranded and twisted silks, Japanese floss silk, fine floss silk, spun (fine twisted) silk.

• COTTON

Most embroiderers are familiar with stranded cotton. It is usually available in six-stranded skeins and strands should be used singly.

• FLOSS SILK

This is untwisted with a high sheen, and is also known as sleave or Japanese silk. It should be doubled or split (as appropriate to the type chosen) to match the gauge of one strand of stranded cotton to complete most of the projects in this book.

• TWISTED SILK

This usually has several strands twisted together. Single strands of most twisted silks are approximately the same gauge as single strands of stranded cotton and should be used singly. Very fine details should be worked in finer gauges of thread if these are available.

• SYNTHETIC METALLIC THREADS

These are available in many forms in gold, silver and various other colours. The most versatile are several stranded threads which may be used entire where a thick gauge is required, or split into single strands for fine or delicate details.

TOOLS

Basic embroidery tools have remained unchanged for centuries and the essentials are described here.

• EMBROIDERY FRAME

In flat-work embroidery the tension of the background fabric is all important (see Stitch variations, page 131) and it is essential to work on an embroidery frame. Round, tambour hoops are best suited to fine embroidery as they produce an entirely uniform tension. Wooden hoops maintain their tension best. Always use a frame large enough to allow a generous amount of fabric around your design.

• SCISSORS

You will need small scissors for threads, fine and sharp. I use pinking shears for cutting fabric, which helps to prevent fraying. Don't use thread or fabric scissors to cut anything else or you will blunt the blades.

• NEEDLES

These should always be chosen with the specific use of threads and fabrics in mind. 'Embroidery' needles are designed with a long eye and a sharp point. A selection of sizes 5 to 10 are the most useful to have in your needle case. Size 8 is ideal for use with a 'single strand' gauge as discussed above.

• 'REAL' GOLD AND SILVER THREAD

These are usually made using a percentage of real gold or silver. Generally they comprise very narrow strips of leaf or fine metal twisted around a synthetic, cotton or silk core. 'Passing' thread is tightly wound and available in various gauges, the finest of which may be used directly in the needle, the thicker couched down. 'Jap' gold is more loosely wound and is available in a variety of gauges but is usually only suitable for couching.

• BLENDING FILAMENTS

This term encompasses a vast number of specialist threads, but usually refers to threads which are made up of a number of strands of differing types, e.g. a silky thread together with a cellophane or sparkling thread. They may be used entire, or split down into their component parts which may then be used separately.

Floss and twisted silk produce different effects: glossy, as shown on the plant and upper sides of the butterflies' wings, or with the subtler, matt glow illustrated by the underside of the wings. 12.75 x 10.75cm (5 x 4½in)

BASIC TECHNIQUES

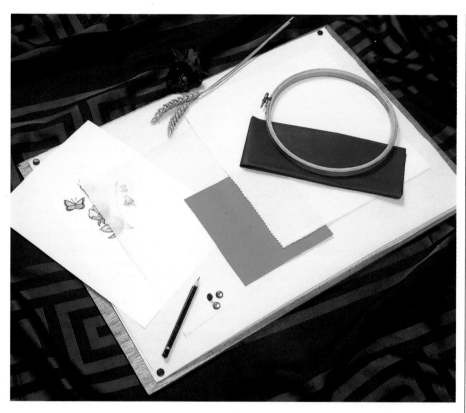

Before you begin to embroider it is important to pay attention to the initial preparation and transfer of your design. Similarly, after your project is completed you need to give some thought to the presentation of the work.

TRANSFERRING A DESIGN

You will need (see picture above, left to right):
- Original design
- Tracing paper
  (use good quality 90gsm)
- 'H' pencil
- Drawing pins
- Dressmakers' carbon paper in a colour contrasting your fabric
- Fabric
- Tissue paper
- Tambour hoop

You will also need scissors and a smooth, hard surface on which to work. Ideally, this should be a wooden drawing board covered with several layers of lining paper.

1 Place the tracing paper over your design and carefully trace off the design, omitting any very fine details, e.g., whiskers, spiders' webs, insects' antennae. These lines, if transferred, could not be covered by single strands of thread and must be added freehand during the course of the embroidery.

2 Lay your fabric flat, and place the tracing on top of it. Pin the tracing in place with two drawing pins at the top right and top left corners. Interleave between fabric and tracing with the carbon (colour side down) and hold secure with a third pin through the tracing at the

bottom of the paper. Do not pin through the carbon.

With a firm, even pressure, re-draw each line of the design. After you have completed a few lines, lift one corner of the tracing and carbon papers to check that the design is transferring successfully.

3 When the transfer is complete, remove the bottom drawing pin, lift back the tracing and remove the carbon paper. Check that every detail of the design has been transferred before finally removing the tracing paper. You are now ready to mount your fabric, using tissue paper and a tambour hoop (see instructions opposite).

MOUNTING FABRIC IN A TAMBOUR HOOP

You will need:
• Fabric, with the design transferred
• Tissue paper
• Tambour hoop

1 Cut two sheets of tissue paper at least 5cm (2in) wider than your hoop. Place the hoop inner ring on a flat surface and lay one sheet of tissue paper over it. Lay your fabric over the paper and ensure that the design is centred in the ring. Lay a second sheet of tissue paper over the fabric and slip the outer ring of the hoop over the entire 'sandwich'. Tighten the screw until held firmly.

2 Trim the upper sheet of tissue paper inside and outside the upper ring (shown above). Turn the hoop over and trim the lower sheet of tissue paper similarly. The tissue paper will protect your fabric from abrasion by the hoop and keep the handled edges clean. You are now ready to begin your embroidery.

MOUNTING AND FRAMING WORK

You will need (see picture above):
• Backing board (rigid cardboard, foamboard or hardboard)
• Acid-free cartridge paper (cut to the same size as the backing board)
• Lacing thread (mercerized cotton is recommended)
• Two crewel needles (large enough to take the chosen cotton)
• Scissors

1 When your embroidery is complete press it on the wrong side, without steam (after checking the manufacturer's instructions for fabric and thread). Always press through another piece of fabric, and be very careful if you have used blending or other specialist filaments, especially cellophane threads.

It is essential to mount your work under similar tension to that exerted upon the fabric whilst in the tambour hoop. Lace it firmly on to a rigid backing board to achieve this tension. Make sure your backing board is large enough to take the whole design, with enough space at each edge to allow for framing.

2 Place the cartridge paper carefully between the board and fabric. Next, position the embroidery, always making sure that the warp/weft of the fabric lies straight in relation the edges of the board.

3 Invert the ensemble so the embroidery is face down, with the cartridge paper and board on top of it. Cut the fabric to size, allowing a comfortable overlap. Fold the two sides in toward the centre of the board. Cut a long but manageable piece of lacing thread and thread a

needle at each end, leaving two 'tails' of similar length.

Working from the top, insert a needle on either side and lace the two sides together, in corset fashion, until you reach the bottom.

4 Fold the top and bottom of the fabric toward the centre and repeat the lacing process. Tie off the ends of the lacing thread with firm, non-slip knots and then snip off any excess thread. It takes a little practise to achieve the perfect tension. Don't over tighten the laces as the thread may break or rip the fabric, but do not be afraid to exert a reasonable pull on the work as only in this way will the original tension of the fabric on the tambour hoop be re-created.

5 The choice of framing is a personal matter, but always be prepared to take professional advice as framing can make or mar a picture. A window mount is a good idea to keep the glass away from the fabric (essential if beads or thick specialist threads have been used) and remember that a frame should complement rather than dominate your design.

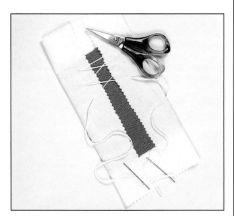

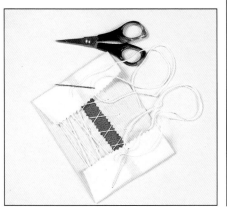

The essence of summer: dog rose and peacock butterfly. 9 x 9cm (3½ x 3½in)

STITCH VARIATIONS

Even a simple study can involve the use of a number of important basic techniques. Here, radial and directional opus plumarium, *stem stitch and straight stitch create a lovely mini-sampler worked in stranded cotton, gold and silver and metallic threads.*
12 x 9.5cm (4¾ x 3¾in)

The stitches used in this book are a combination of traditional embroidery stitches and some contemporary innovations. They are flexible and adaptable: a single stitch such as stem stitch, depending on how it is applied, can produce a variety of effects, from a fine, sinuous line to a broad, strong one, with an infinite choice of widths, curves and reflexes within each variation.

The stitches fall into distinct types: linear, filling and decorative. Each has its own special properties and is suited to the description of certain shapes, fields and textures.

When working on a hoop the fabric must be taut within the frame. Stitches are always worked by the 'stab and pull' method. The needle is pushed through the fabric from above, the embroiderer's hand then moves to the back and pulls the needle through the fabric so the stitch forms smoothly on the surface. The next stitch is begun by pushing the needle up through the fabric from the reverse of the work, the hand brought to the front to pull the needle through, prior to beginning the routine once again.

LINEAR STITCHES
1 STEM STITCH
Always work from the top of any line to be described (on a natural history subject the outer extremity). Work with the curve of the subject: bring your needle out just to the outside of the curve and put it in on the inside of the curve.

a Fine/narrow stem stitch
Overlap the stitches by only a small proportion of the stitch length. The line created is only the width of a single stitch, creating a fine, sinuous effect.

b Broad stem stitch
Overlap the stitches so that half to three-quarters of each stitch lies beside its neighbour. The juxtaposition of several stitches creates a thick, strong effect.

c Graduating stem stitch

Begin with a fine stem stitch, increase it to a one-half ratio, then to three-quarters ratio within the same line creating the effect of a gradually thickening line (such as describes a growing stem – narrower at the tip, broader at the base).

d Coiling stem stitch

Begin coiling stem stitch with small stitches to describe the tight curve at the centre of the coil and gradually lengthen the stitches as the curve becomes gentler.

e Reflexing stem stitch

Beginning at the tip of the line, work the chosen variation a–c until the direction of the curve begins to change. Take one straight stitch through the preceding stitch, directly along the pattern line. Begin the stem stitch again, bringing the needle up on the new outside of the curve.

2 STRAIGHT STITCH

There are occasions when a completely straight line in the pattern can be described by a simple straight stitch, or when a large field of the design must be filled smoothly with abutting straight stitches, such as in landscape work. The fabric must be taut within your frame to work this technique successfully.

a Vertical straight stitch (long)

Work this stitch from the top downward. Usually the stitches will be angled toward their base, such as in the case of simple grass effects. Ensure the stitch completely covers the transfer line.

b Horizontal straight stitch (long)

This stitch is used in blocks to suggest landscape effects. Work toward any abutting groups of stitches. To suggest a break in perspective, void (see 4, right) between abutting fields. To blend shades within a single field, stitch into the abutting field.

c Free straight stitch (long or short)

Fine details, such as whiskers, do not appear as transferred pattern lines (see Basic techniques, page 128). These can be worked freehand in straight stitches angled to suit the particular needs of the subject matter. Work away from abutting groups of stitches.

3 SHADOW LINING

Establish the direction of the imagined light source within your picture. Each element of the design away from this light source will be shadow lined. Put a pin in the work, tip pointing in the light source direction, to remind you of its origin.

a Smooth shadow lining

This is achieved by working a fine, accurate stem stitch along the pattern line, just to its underside.

b Fragmented shadow lining

Where a line is too irregular to permit shadow lining by stem stitch, use straight stitches, tailoring these to the length of the section of outline to be described.

4 VOIDING

Where two fields of a filling technique abut (see opposite), with or without a shadow line, suggesting that one element of the design overlaps another, a narrow line void of stitching should be left between the two. In practice, this forms on the transferred pattern line, dividing the two elements. It should be approximately as wide as the gauge of thread used for the embroidery itself. To check that the width is correct, loosely position a strand of the thread along the 'valley' of the void. If the thread fits snugly, the width is correct.

SPLIT STITCH

Between true linear stitches and filling stitches comes split stitch, a hybrid technique that dates from the Anglo-Saxon era. Single lines of split stitch can be created by working directly on to the transferred outline of the design, each short, straight stitch splitting the preceding stitch by bringing the needle up through it. By working lines of split stitch closely abutting, the fabric or ground can be completely covered, thus creating a filling technique.

FILLING STITCHES

I OPUS PLUMARIUM

This Latin term literally means 'a work of feathers' and emulates the way in which feathers lie smoothly, yet with infinite changes of direction, upon a bird's body. The angle of the stitches sweeps around without breaking the flow of the stitching itself, and this in turn catches the light, refracting it back from the stitching, to give one of the most realistic three-dimensional impressions you can achieve in embroidery.

a Radial opus plumarium
(*single or first stratum*)

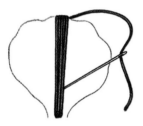

Begin with a stitch central to the field to be covered. This, and all subsequent stitches, are worked from the outer edge of the pattern line inwards toward the centre of the motif. Bring the needle out adjacent to the top of the first stitch. Slip the needle beneath the first stitch and through the fabric about two-thirds of the way down its length. This advances the angle of the stitching.

Subsequent stitches can be full length or shorter and angled as described, allowing the embroidery to fan out and cover the field without too many stitches bunching at the inner core. A gradual advancement of the angle is achieved by working the angled stitches longer (e.g., three-quarters of the length of full stitches); more acute advancement by working them shorter (a quarter to a half of the length of the full stitches).

b Radial opus plumarium
(*subsequent strata*)

Where a broad field of stitches is required to fill a motif, several strata of *opus plumarium* may be needed. Work the first stratum using the single stratum method described above. Always stitching inwards (towards the core of the motif), work the second stratum by taking a first stitch at the centre of the field to be filled. Stitch into the first stratum (do not leave a void) and, following the established flow of the stitching, fan out on either side of the first stitch, advancing the angle when necessary, as before. Subsequent strata are worked in a similar fashion.

c Directional opus plumarium
(*single or first stratum*)

Where the core of the motif is elongated (e.g., the central vein of an elliptic leaf) the stitches should flow smoothly along its length. Always stitch inwards, bringing the needle out at the motif's edge and in toward its centre. Begin at the tip of the motif (or outer extremity of the first stratum) and take the first stitch inwards to abut the tip of the elongated core. Work your way down the field advancing the angle, as described above (a).

d Directional opus plumarium
(*subsequent strata*)

Work the first strata as above. Again working from the direction of the motif's tip inwards, create subsequent strata by stitching into the previous stratum (do not void), advancing the angle to match the abutting stitches.

2 OPPOSITE ANGLE STITCHING

This is used to create the effect of reflex, e.g., where a leaf or petal curls forwards or backwards to reveal its underside.

Following the principles of *opus plumarium* work the stitches at an exactly opposite angle to the abutting field. (Occasionally the angles will be similar in actuality, but opposite in relation to the concept of the directional stitching.) Where necessary void between the two.

3 SNAKE STITCH

This is used to describe long, sinuous shapes, such as broad blades of grass or other linear leaves.

a Simple snake stitch

Begin at the tip of the motif, taking the first stitch in the direction of the curve to be described.

For subsequent stitches, bring the needle out on the outside of the curve and in on the inside. Work smoothly down the motif, advancing the angle of stitches, if necessary, by the *opus plumarium* method and lengthening the stitches where appropriate, as with graduating stem stitch (see page 132).

b Reflexing snake stitch

Begin at the point of reflex, where the direction of the curve changes. Firstly, take a stitch angled across the field slanting between the tip and base of the curve. Work upwards to the tip, bringing the needle out on the outside of the curve and in on the inside until the upper field is complete. Advance the angle of stitching by the *opus plumarium* method if necessary. Complete the lower field by returning to the central stitch and working down the motif, again bringing the needle out on the outside and in on the inside of the curve. Advance the stitch angle as necessary.

4 DALMATIAN DOG TECHNIQUE

This is used to create a single, smooth field of embroidery where an area of one colour is completely encompassed by another colour. It is used within *opus plumarium* (either radial or directional).

a Simple Dalmatian dog

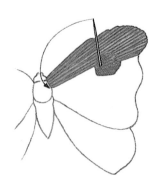

Establish the radial or directional flow of the *opus plumarium*. Working the stitches at exactly the same angle as the main field of *opus plumarium* to follow, work the spots or other fields to be covered first. When completed, flood the rest of the *opus plumarium* around them, again paying careful attention to the flow of the stitches.

b Multiple Dalmatian dog

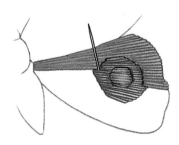

This technique can create a 'spot within a spot' or any other irregular pattern.

Establish either the radial or directional flow of the *opus plumarium*. Maintaining the angle of stitching as above, work the innermost colour first, followed by outer field or fields of colour until the spots or other shapes are complete. Flood the surrounding *opus plumarium* around them.

DECORATIVE STITCHES

1 SEED STITCH

Fine, short, straight stitches worked directly on to the fabric, occasionally superimposed over other embroidery.

2 TICKING

These are seed stitches overlaying *opus plumarium*. They are worked at exactly the same angle as the underlying work but are taken in the opposite direction, i.e., against the flow of the work.

3 STUDDING

These are seed stitches that overlay *opus plumarium*. The stitches are worked at right angles to the underlying stitches.

4 SHOOTING STITCH

Long straight stitches taken in the opposite direction to the underlying radial or directional work.

5 CHEVRON STITCH

Two long straight stitches are angled to meet. Infill with a third straight stitch if necessary. To create a very sharp angle (such as a thistle spike) work a fourth straight stitch in a fine gauge of thread through the body of the motif.

6 DOTTING/SPECKLING

Work dotting and speckling in very short straight stitches, only as long as the width of the thread, to create an impression of tiny round dots. Work the stitches close together and in random directions.

7 FLOATING EMBROIDERY

This technique allows the threads to lie loosely on the fabric, falling into attractive, spontaneous shapes. Do not transfer the design to be formed on to the background fabric but suggest only the outer periphery of the pattern with a few lightly transferred dots.

Take a long stitch from the inside to the outside of the motif, putting a finger, pencil or other implement under the thread to keep it away from the fabric. Take a very small stitch at the outer point of the motif to bring the thread back to the surface. Take a third stitch back to the core of the motif, again keeping a finger beneath the thread to maintain the distance. Repeat the process, removing the finger or pencil when several strands have built up.

8 SURFACE COUCHING

Usually a goldwork technique, this can be used on various threads.

Bring the thread to be couched (the base thread) through the fabric to the surface of the work. If it is too thick to be brought through the fabric, lay it in place and hold it down with a thumb. Thread a second needle with a finer thread (the couching thread) and bring it up through the fabric immediately alongside the base thread. Take a tiny stitch over the base thread, at right angles to it, and repeat at regular intervals, effectively using the couching thread to whip the base thread into place along the transferred pattern line. Pay particular attention to whipping the beginning and the end of the base thread into place if it is lying wholly on the surface of the work.

9 SUBDUED VOIDING

Where two fields of *opus plumarium* abut and are separated by a voided line, the effect can be softened by working fine straight stitches, at the angle of the underlying work, across the void. Use a shade similar to that of the embroidered field 'closer' in perspective to the viewer, for example, where a bird's wing lies over its body, or the angle of its neck creates a break in perspective. Work the overlying stitches at regular intervals, allowing the voided line to show through.

SUPPLIERS

There are many manufacturers and suppliers of embroidery materials and equipment and I have suggested a few here.

An asterisk indicates suppliers who will accept orders direct from the given address via mail order.

Coats Crafts UK
PO Box 22, The Lingfield Estate,
McMullen Road, Darlington,
Co. Durham DL1 1YQ, UK
tel: 01325 365457
Stranded cottons

Coats and Clark
Susan Bates Inc., 30 Patewood Drive,
Greenville, SC 29615, USA
tel: (US) 800 241 5997
Stranded cottons

DMC Creative World Ltd.
Pullman Road, Wigston,
Leicestershire LE18 2DY, UK
tel: 0116 281 1040
website: www.dmc/cw.com
Stranded cotton, imitation gold
and silver thread

Helen M. Stevens
Lectures, masterclasses
and themed holidays are available
based around Helen's work.
For full details check her
website: www.helenmstevens.co.uk
Alternatively, contact Helen via
David & Charles, Brunel House,
Newton Abbot, Devon,
TQ12 4PU, UK.

DMC Corporation
Building 10, Port Kearny,
South Kearny, NJ 07032, USA
tel: (US) 201 589 0606
Stranded cotton, imitation gold
and silver thread

*Japanese Embroidery Centre UK **
White Lodge, Littlewick Road,
Lower Knaphill, Woking,
Surrey GU21 2JU, UK
tel: 01483 476246
Floss silk, real gold and silver threads,
imitation gold, silver and metallic threads

Kreinik Manufacturing Co. Inc.
3106 Timanus Lane, Suite 101,
Baltimore, MD 21244, USA
tel: (US) 800 537 2166
(UK 01325 365 457)
website: www.kreinik.com
email: kreinik@kreinik.com
Blending filaments and metallic threads

Madeira Threads (UK) Ltd.
PO Box 6, Thirsk,
North Yorkshire YO7 3BX, UK
tel: 01845 524880
email: acts@madeira
website: www.madeira.co.uk
Twisted/stranded silks and cottons

Pearsall's
Tancrad Street, Taunton,
Somerset TA1 1RY, UK
tel: 01823 274700
website: www.pearsallsembroidery.co.uk
Stranded pure silk thread

*Pipers Specialist Silks **
Chinnerys, Egremont Street,
Glemsford, Sudbury,
Suffolk C110 7SA, UK
tel: 01787 280920
website: www.pipers-silks.com
email: susanpeck@pipers-silks.com
Floss and spun (twisted) silk.
Exclusive silk kits designed by Helen M.
Stevens including Plate 20 pansy, page 30
and Plate 58 red admiral, page 89

*Stephen Simpson Ltd. **
50 Manchester Road, Preston,
Lancashire PR1 3YH, UK
tel: 01772 556688
Real gold and silver threads

*The Voirrey Embroidery Centre **
Brimstage Hall,
Wirral CH63 6JA, UK
tel: 0151 3423514
website: www.voirrey.com
General embroidery supplies

ACKNOWLEDGMENTS

I am grateful to the following clients for permission to include their pictures in this book:

Plate 1 first appeared in	Stitch with The Embroiderer's Guild	Plate 22	Mrs R. Abraham	Plate 48	Helen Hill
Plate 11	Christina Leslau	Plate 28	Shirley Chard	Plate 55 & 56	Peter and Joan Boughton
Plate 20 & 58	Sue Peck	Plate 32	Joanne Pitchers	Plate 65	Miss M. Joynson
Plate 21	Wing. Cdr. D. and Mrs M. Bennett	Plate 33	Ann Duddridge	Plate 68	Irene Barnes
		Plate 47	Betty Bone	Page 130	Hannah Sophia Kemp

Without the support of friends and family (my parents in particular) – who saw me only occasionally when I was in 'writing mode'! – this book would not have been written. Nigel and Angela Salmon have been marvellous advisors throughout on matters of presentation, and David & Charles, as ever, model publishers! I am grateful to Cheryl Brown and all the in-house team and to Lin Clements for her intuitive editing skills. My thanks also to my marvellous PA Pam Crossley for taking the load of other matters off my shoulders! Love and thanks to you all.

INDEX